In this book, leading textile artist Jean Draper explores how structure in both the built and the natural environment can inspire and inform the design and construction of stitched textiles. The work begins with study and research and then develops through work in thread, stitch, cloth and other materials to create new structures. Through a series of exploratory stages (beginning with thread and concluding with fabric) the author shows how the formations we see around us can be interpreted and represented in textile art. These can be two-dimensional structural surfaces made from stitching, or more complex three-dimensional constructions made from either stitch alone or from a combination of stitching, fabric and mixed media.

Both machine and hand stitching techniques are covered, with easy-to-follow instructions and diagrams for more unusual methods and examples of experimental stitched textiles and structures made with stitched fabrics. Illustrated throughout with examples of the author's work as well as that of other textile artists, this beautiful book will inspire you to experiment with your own stitched structures.

STITCH AND STRUCTURE

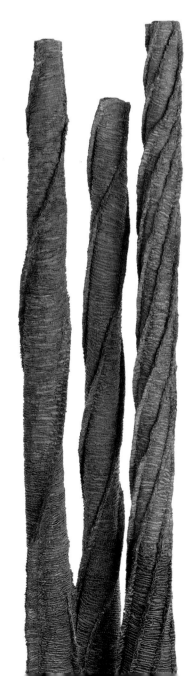

STITCH AND STRUCTURE

JEAN DRAPER

BATSFORD

For Ken and Matthew

First published in the United Kingdom in
2013 by
Batsford
10 Southcombe Street
London W14 0RA
An imprint of Anova Books Company Ltd

ISBN:9781849941211

A CIP catalogue record for this book is
available from the British Library.

10 9 8 7 6 5 4 3 2 1

Repro by Rival Colour, UK
Printed and bound by Craft Print
International Ltd,Singapore

This book can be ordered direct from
the publisher at the website:
www.anovabooks.com
or try your local bookshop.

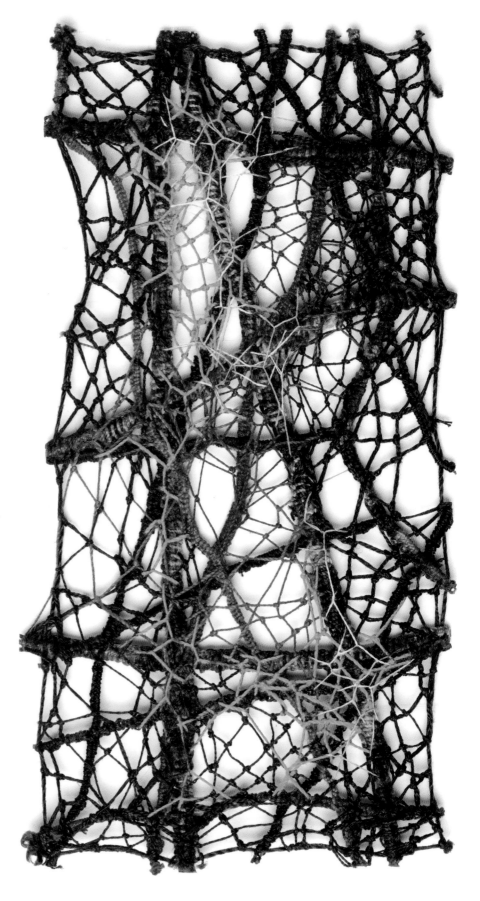

Right Lacy structure worked on soluble fabric.
Layers of knotted stitching with covered wire
supports. See Chapter 5.

CONTENTS

INTRODUCTION

This book has grown out of many years of practising, researching and teaching art and stitched textiles. It is solidly based in my continuing work around themes and textile techniques that interest me. While my natural way of working is hand stitching – and this is the way much of the work shown in this book has been made – some pieces are machine stitched. Many of the hand-stitching ideas shown could also be translated as machine embroidery.

In these pages, I aim to explore how structure in the natural and built environment can offer inspiration for the design and construction of stitched textiles. As artists, embroiderers and makers, we can use these structures to shape our vision and to make that vision a reality through the ways in which we work with thread, stitch, cloth and other materials. Through a series of logical exploratory stages (beginning with thread and concluding with fabric) and based on the design concept of structure, I attempt to show how formations we see around us can be interpreted and represented in our chosen materials and methods which, in turn, allows us to create new structures. These can be very varied: different two-dimensional structural surfaces made from stitching, or more complex three-dimensional constructions fashioned either from stitch alone or from stitching, fabric and mixed media combined. Shown here is my progress so far in this immense subject.

The overriding principle during my teaching career has been to encourage creative growth in others, giving them the opportunity to develop their own ideas and personal style of working. I certainly do not want to prescribe the outcomes of your work, but by suggesting starting points and possible additional working experiments you might carry out (under the heading 'Further Work: You Could…'), my intention is to inspire and encourage you to develop interesting ideas for yourself.

I have chosen only to illustrate and explain those methods that you may not already know or be able to reference easily. I have stated where my ideas begin and how my methods have evolved, in the knowledge that you can easily source basic information about stitches and techniques from the many good specialist books already in existence.

I hope that you will enjoy reading and using this book and that it will help you to make expressive, individual and innovative work of your own.

Right *After the Fire* (54 x 38cm). Hand-stitched background in dense vertical lines of raised whip stitch (see p120), supporting an arrangement of wrapped sticks, thorns, stitched and painted hand-made paper and loose threads. Constructed from cotton fabric, various threads and mixed media.

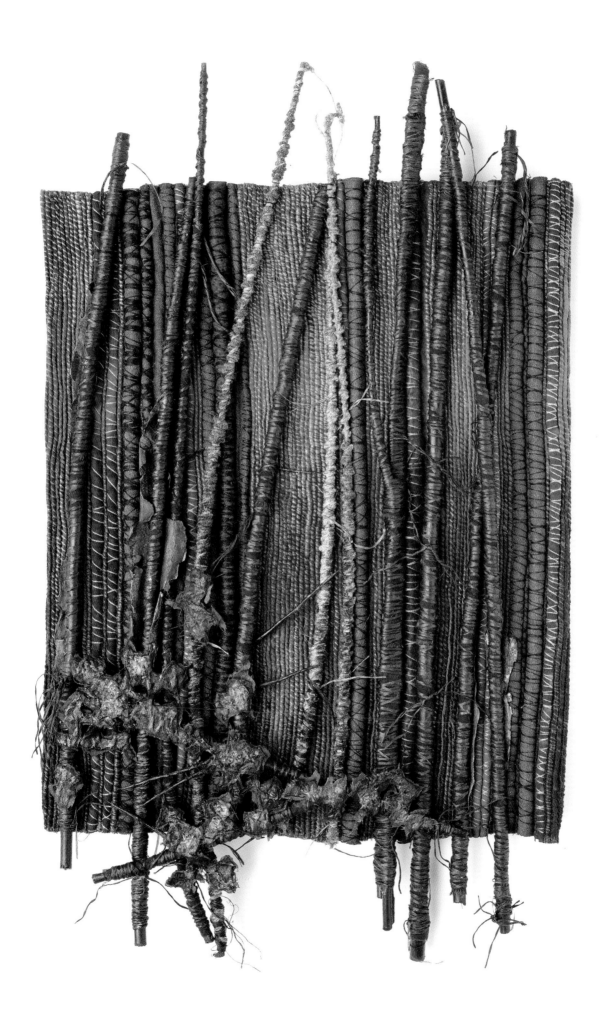

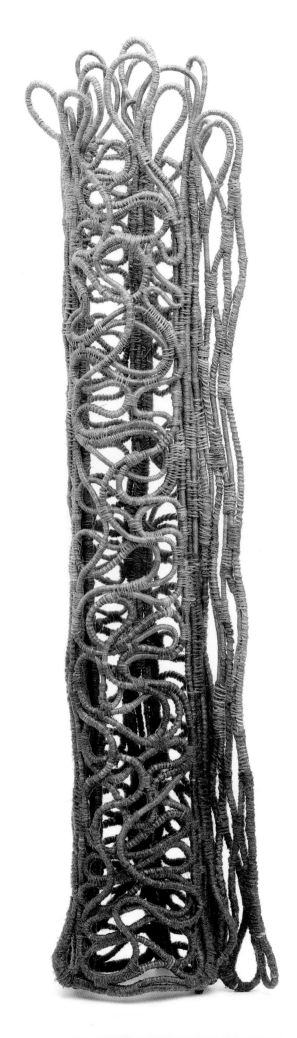

DISCOVERING STRUCTURE AS A SOURCE FOR DESIGN

Defining structure. Natural structures.
Man-made structures. Increasing awareness
of structure in the environment.

Left *Cactus Form 1* (height 58cm). Tall three-
dimensional work constructed from heavy cords
wrapped with space-dyed cotton threads, based
on drawings of dried cacti shown later on pages
22 and 74. For method of construction see
Chapter 5.

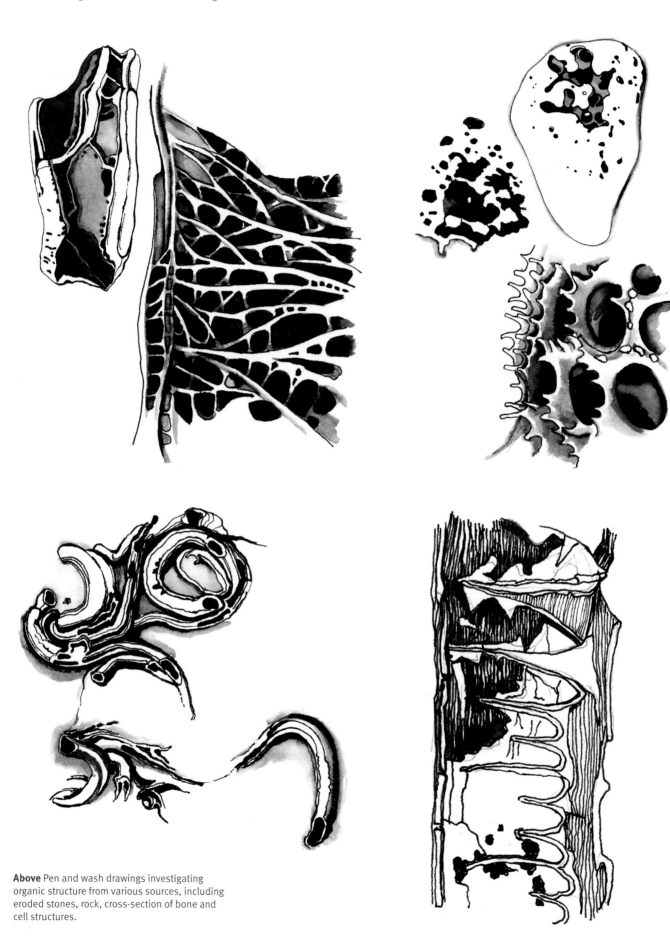

Above Pen and wash drawings investigating organic structure from various sources, including eroded stones, rock, cross-section of bone and cell structures.

ORGANIC OR NATURAL STRUCTURE

'Structure can be defined in a number of ways, but it is generally accepted that the term refers to the framework or constituent parts or elements making up an object. It also refers to the way in which these parts are put together and connected, determining the particular nature, character and shape of the object.'

The Shorter Oxford English Dictionary

There has been a great deal of study into, and writing on, the theory and science of structure which, while interesting, is not essential reading for the purposes of this book. Here we are only beginning to explore structure in a general way as an aid to the creation of stitched textiles. However, more in-depth research might be needed if you wished to develop very complex work, particularly if you are thinking of making large-scale standing structures. Size in relation to the strength and weight of the materials used would need careful consideration. At this stage, however, we are predominately concerned with discovering the visual impact and inspirational qualities of structure in its broader sense. Whatever its form, every living, growing thing around us has some kind of structure that affects its appearance and determines its shape, size, strength and character. The structure of some objects is immediately recognizable, being on the exterior or surface, while less obvious interior structures are hidden and, therefore, are more difficult to discover. Outwardly, for example, the human body seems to be made from muscle and flesh, but our shape, strength and ability to stand and move is largely dependent upon the concealed bony skeleton that supports the muscles and soft tissue and also protects the inner organs. By contrast, some creatures, such as shellfish, turtles and insects, have a bold, protective outer shell or carapace instead of an interior skeleton. You will be able to think of many more examples of both surface and interior structures in the things you see around you.

Essentially, the structure – the way in which the elements relate, conjoin and shape an entity – is entirely practical in order to give strength, flexibility and protection. Its structure enables an object to exist and hold intact against whatever forces and dangers may affect it in its environment.

Organic structures – interior or exterior – although primarily practical, can also be very decorative and intriguing in their form, construction and coloration. Often, exterior decoration serves a practical purpose too, perhaps to attract a mate, or for the benefit of camouflage. The complexity and variety of structures within nature can supply us with almost unlimited information and inspiration, providing compelling scope for interesting design. Some structures, when examined closely, seem impossibly delicate but, in fact, because of the way in which their elements, (often including a framework of lines) are organized, linked and overlapped, together with the way they function in their environment, the fineness and lightness we see belies their strength. Examples of this type of structure are cobwebs and the inner lacy construction of bones. In fact, many fascinating structures, such as cells and other biological organisms, are so minute and fine that they are completely invisible to the naked eye and only become apparent through magnification. Nevertheless, some of these forms provide very beautiful and exciting starting points for stitch.

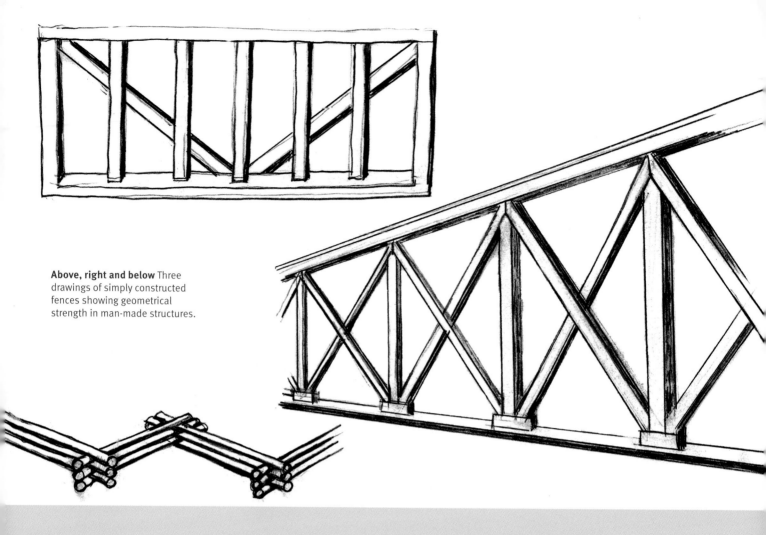

Above, right and below Three drawings of simply constructed fences showing geometrical strength in man-made structures.

FURTHER WORK: YOU COULD...

Begin by looking around and making yourself aware of organic or natural structures. These could include:

Plant stems (outside and cross sections); trees (the whole branching shape; details of tree bark, roots, etc.); the skin and scales of different animals, e.g. insects, fish and snakes; shells; cell structures; crystals and minerals; nests; webs, fruits and seeds (outside and in cross section), skeletal structures and rocks (surface details and whole formations).

BUILT OR MAN-MADE STRUCTURES

From earliest times, human beings have studied, learned and drawn from the strength and variety in natural structures in order to help them create and develop the kind of practical and robust structures needed for their own use. Initially, the priority was to provide protection and shelter and simply sustain existence but, subsequently, the same principles were applied to both buildings and other structures with more complex and varied functions. In architecture, for example, simple timber frames using trees and branches were used firstly to support soft building materials such as straw, twigs, leaves and mud to make basic shelters. Later, as building became more advanced, timber frames, still reflecting and imitating the original strong growth structure of trees, were used to support hard materials such as stone and fired clay bricks. It is thought that similar structural knowledge of trees was employed in the construction of the pillars and arches supporting mighty cathedrals built entirely from stone.

Many other examples exist that show natural structures inspiring man-made ones.

MAN MADE

By studying how structure works in nature, people have been able to understand how fragile, lightweight structures can have enormous strength and durability. In his book *Origins of Form*, Christopher Williams has written:

> Structure is the way to achieve the most strength from the least material through the most appropriate arrangement of elements within the form for the intended use…

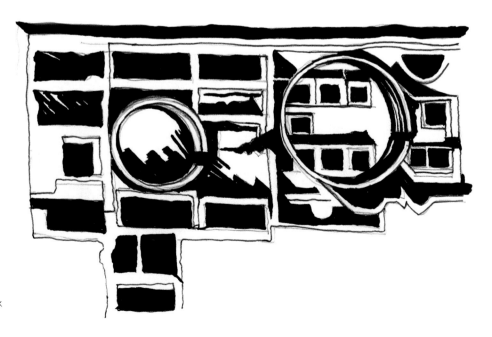

Right *Man-made Structure*. Pen, brush and ink drawing illustrating simple geometric forms, seen from above, in Pueblo ruins, Arizona.

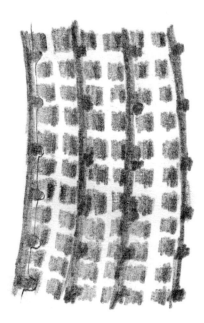

He also emphasizes the importance of economy in structure, arguing that you cannot necessarily make something strong by building mass or volume. Birds' wings are a very good example: without economy in the structure of the wing, the bird could not fly because it would be too heavy. Similarly, the aeroplane, developed originally from the study of flight in birds, uses economy of structure together with increasing structural knowledge of metals, to create strength and lightness relative to size.

SQUARES OR TRIANGLES

We are surrounded by man-made structures, ranging from the simplest to highly sophisticated examples of structural engineering, many of which have their earliest roots in Man's ability to observe and learn from nature which are the strongest shapes and to understand the way in which the elements in organic forms join and hold together. Christopher Williams points out that man-made structures are often composed of a simplification of the forms found in nature: circles and domes, squares, rectangles and triangles, the most common being the triangle. It is repeated many times in both natural and man-made structures because of its basic stability.

Above Drawings from shells and rocks showing squares and rectangles in nature.

Right Drawings from rocks and rock strata showing triangles in nature.

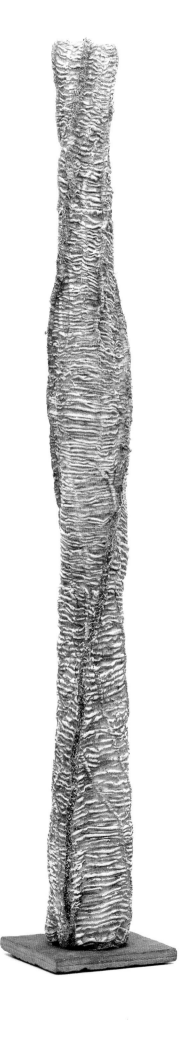

FURTHER WORK: YOU COULD...

Continue to look around and become more aware of man-made structures in the environment. These could include:

Fences (old and new); gates; scaffolding; ladders; wheels; buildings (old and contemporary, inside and outside); architectural features – arches, windows, stairs, etc.; furniture; lamps; lights; chandeliers; baskets; boxes; cartons; contemporary sculpture and ceramics.

Can you see any relationship between these and the natural structures you have found?

Left *Rock Form* (height 60cm) Tall structure made from machine-stitched, dyed and painted cotton fabric with external seams. Supported on armature and a slate base.

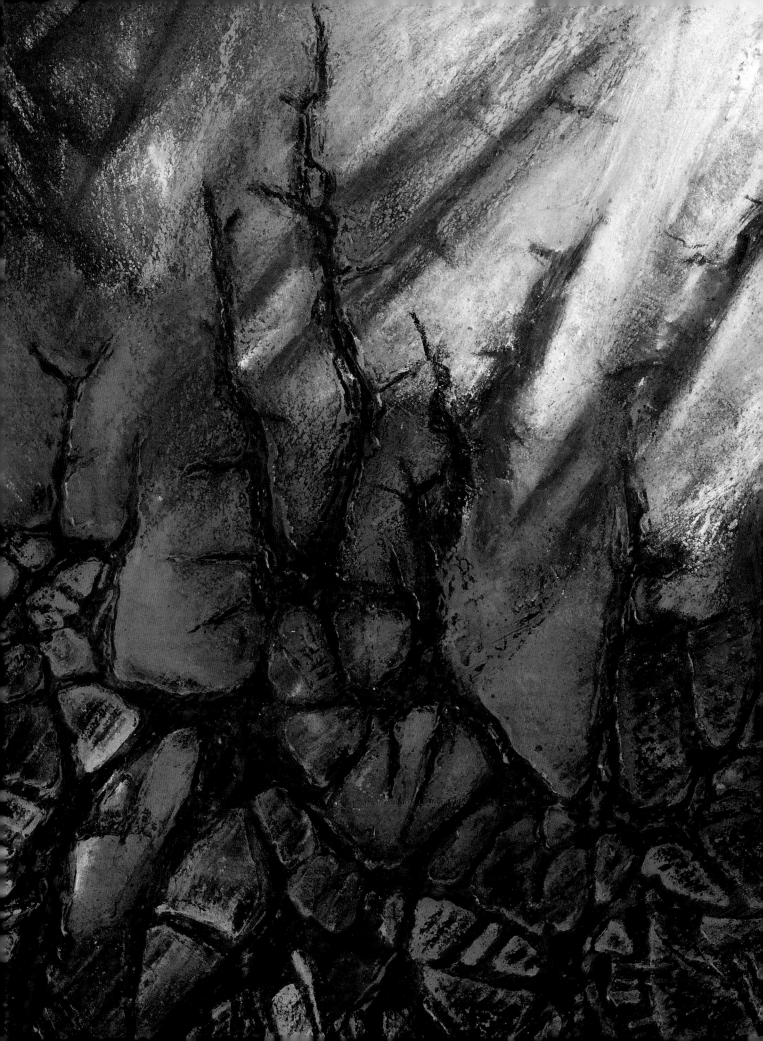

AN APPROACH TO MAKING EXPERIMENTAL STITCHED TEXTILES

Recording information about structure for translation into stitch. Drawing with a purpose. Compiling your own database of knowledge for informing your work.

Left Detail of pastel drawing recording dramatic, twisted tree structures remaining after a wild fire.

While the main focus of this book is the exploration of structure through stitch, alongside this I have tried to demonstrate the working process of developing ideas by gathering and simplifying information, translating this information into stitch through sampling, which leads eventually to resolved stitched textiles. I hope that my drawings, extensive sampling of ideas and examples of finished work, will show you that making work is not so much a mystical procedure but a sound practical system that is ongoing and develops gradually over a period of time; a way of working that can be adopted by most dedicated makers. Ideas for work do not have to be separate and distinct but they develop little by little, one from another; sometimes there is only a small step between them. This should be evident by the related nature of some of the work shown here.

My work process could be simplified under the following headings:
* Looking/Recording/Learning
* Experimental Sampling
* Resolved Work.

But, in fact, the path is never a straightforward one and I find that I constantly need to switch back and forth between the different activities, perhaps when I find I do not have enough information about my subject, or when the methods and materials I am using do not allow me to resolve work satisfactorily.

Even though knowledge and practice of method is invaluable, it is my belief that the strongest work in stitched textiles does not begin with technique alone but with an imaginative eye for inspirational subject matter. As suggested in the previous chapter, it is important to develop an interested and informed way of looking at things that surround us, noticing specific details such as colour, texture, pattern and shape. The emotional response experienced to a particular aspect of our surroundings, and the motivation to express something about it, can lead to the most exciting and individual work.

The process of looking, gathering and recording information by drawing, photography, making notes, reading and making samples is crucial. This research leads to greater understanding of subject matter and the gradual release and generation of more and more ideas. It is enormously beneficial to have your own personal reference material that can be constantly consulted and also updated as more is learned and discovered.

Your source material will not only provide direct visual information to inspire your work, but (specially important for structure), it will show how parts connect, join and support each other to make sustainable forms, as described in the last chapter. Using this information helps in the successful practical construction of work as well as providing ideas that can help create an attractive appearance. You will need this in order to help you construct your pieces with strength and style.

Above Pastel drawing of fallen and leaning trees left after a wild fire in the American southwest.

Left Complete drawing from which the detail on page 16 was taken.

LOOKING AND RECORDING

In a recent interview, the artist David Hockney said that we have to learn to look. Then, in order to understand what we are looking at, we have to ask ourselves the right questions. It is only then that we can begin to engage with our subject and record our interpretation of it. In this section I shall try to describe my approach to this process.

PHOTOGRAPHS

For many people, photographs are possibly the most immediate source of inspiration. In fact, some subject matter (for example, microscopic or biological structures as described in the previous chapter) can often only be sourced through photographs in books or perhaps on the Internet. But photographs alone do not tell the whole story and, although I frequently use photographs, I like to use them in conjunction with drawing and making notes.

I prefer not to attempt to copy a photograph but, instead, to use it as a starting point for my own interpretation of the subject matter. Drawing a small section of the photograph, enlarging it, enhancing parts that interest you particularly, all lead to more individual results. Working this way, perhaps cutting up the photographic image, also enables us to break away from the regular, recognizable proportion and format.

Rather than taking many photographs in an indiscriminate manner, it is an advantage to be selective and to use the camera with great care, in conjunction with careful looking.

A small notebook/sketchbook, with plain paper, is an essential piece of equipment that goes everywhere with me and I would be lost if it went missing. I use this book at odd times, wherever I am, to jot down my reaction to things that interest me, or thoughts about subject matter. I often begin with words and brief phrases to describe what I am seeing and also to embed the most important points in my mind. These notes make the connection between what I am seeing around me and my own ongoing work. I usually make swift drawings – a form of visual note taking – in the same book. I sometimes add cuttings, photographs and other bits of relevant information. I can then go on to make more considered drawings at a later time.

If you do not already keep notes and drawings, I can only strongly urge you to do so because by recording in words, drawings, diagrams and also photographs, you are essentially assembling a vocabulary, or database, of information necessary for your work.

In order to demonstrate that there are many ways to approach drawing, those shown throughout this book, from my sketchbooks, are purposely selected to show the use of a variety of drawing media and styles. As already explained, my drawing, gathering of information and making processes are intertwined so it is impossible, and not necessarily relevant, to place every drawing alongside a piece of work. I hope that you will be able to recognise the connections between the drawings in various parts of the book, the emphasis on certain subject matter and finished work illustrated.

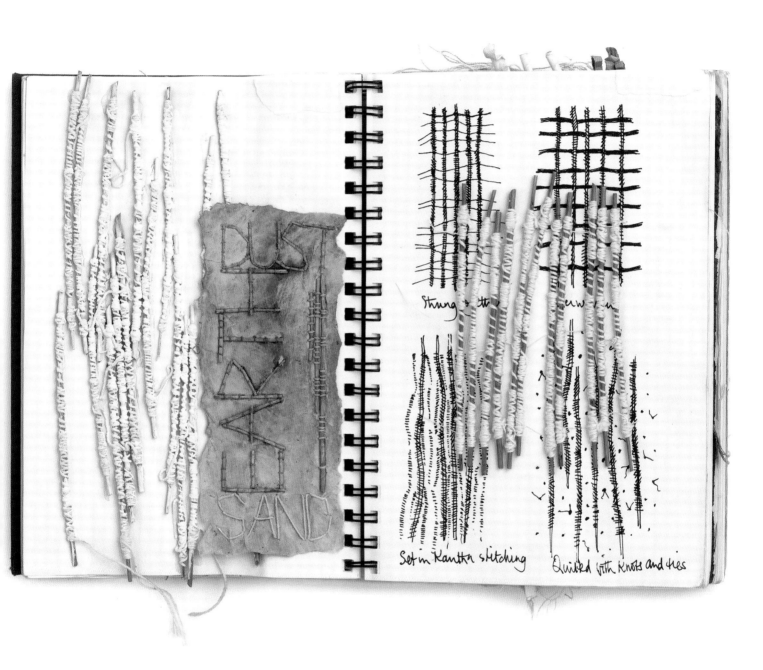

Above Photograph of a double-page spread in a notebook/sketchbook showing a combination of drawings, stitching and wrapped sticks, recording ideas for the development of structured surfaces.

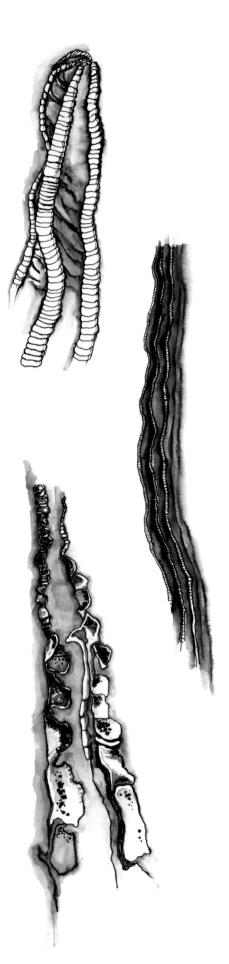

DRAWING WITH A PURPOSE

Some people are nervous of drawing, but I encourage everyone to try. If you study something carefully enough to draw it, perhaps diagrammatically, you will notice much more than a glance or even a photograph will reveal and you will gain and retain much more information to help you with design.

Should you feel reluctant to draw because you feel that you lack the skill to do it well, it is worth reminding yourself that you are drawing with a particular purpose in mind – that of gathering information for your own use, rather than attempting to create masterpieces to be framed. You do not need to show your drawings, or explain them, to other people: they are for you alone, to jog your memory about something you have seen that might possibly form the starting point of work in stitched textiles.

It is often unnecessary to attempt to represent the whole object or shape unless it is of particular interest. Instead, I suggest you concentrate on the details that interest you. Try making several small studies of what you see within the object, concentrating on details of lines, shapes, textures and structure. Rather than just one drawing leading to an individual piece of work, my many small investigative drawings help to establish and confirm characteristic structures, shapes and rhythms in the object.

Looking hard and drawing is an intense process requiring concentration, and to help I often ask myself questions. Examples of my internal dialogue may be seen in the list of points at the end of this chapter (see page 31).

By making small studies in this way, I almost immediately see possibilities for translation into fabric and thread and I think you will do so too. Of course, you will not see actual stitches, but you will probably see marks and shapes that remind you of certain stitches and methods and certainly suggest the weight and thickness of thread you might use.

Work then gradually evolves from the collection of information that has been absorbed.

Above and opposite above
Pen-and-wash drawings of
cacti, informing threads in
Chapter 3 and other cacti
structures.

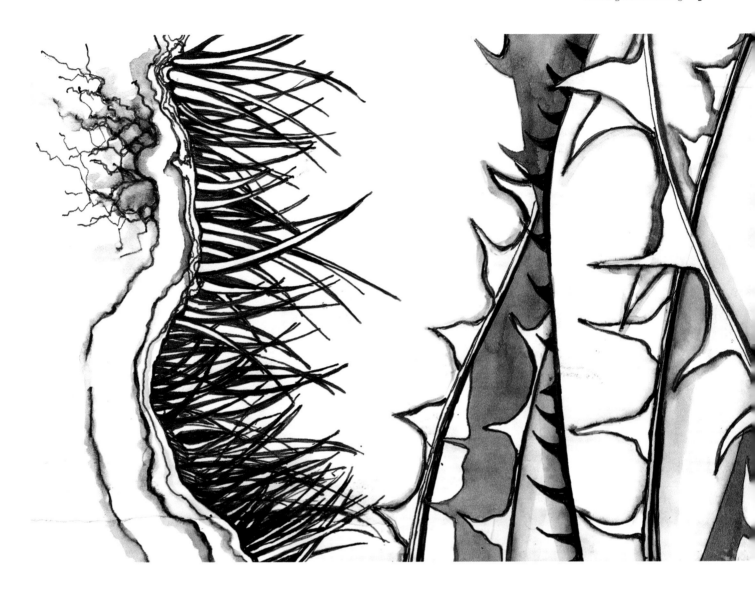

Below Group of drawings
showing stitch ideas suggested
by natural structures.

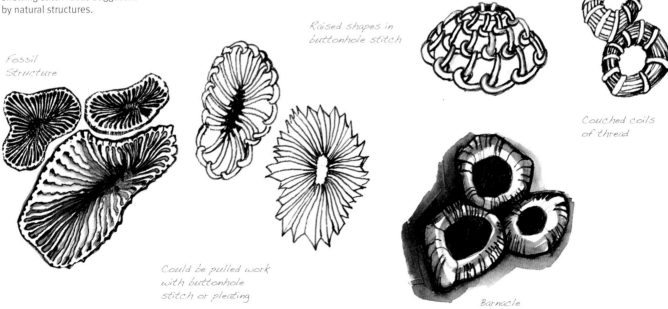

Fossil
Structure

Raised shapes in
buttonhole stitch

Couched coils
of thread

Could be pulled work
with buttonhole
stitch or pleating

Barnacle

METHODS AND TECHNIQUES

Most of the techniques explored in this book are traditional ones that I have altered by changing the usual scale associated with them, by working them more freely and, in some cases, experimenting with new and different materials. Although I believe it is always important to make well-crafted work, the expressive, sculptural approach I have adopted for a while now often necessitates abandoning regularity and the generally accepted size of stitching as shown in most stitch dictionaries and method books. I have learned not to think of 'right' or 'wrong' but to ask myself if I am achieving the effect I am striving for in the interpretation of my design ideas and if the manner of working is acceptable in finish.

TAKING RISKS

Alongside developing an understanding of the subject or source material, the second essential is a mind open to imaginative experimentation. The willingness to try out ideas, to take risks with materials, even precious ones, and being unafraid to make mistakes, is a great advantage. While I would not want to waste anything deliberately, I have found that, in sampling ideas, I can only substitute cheaper materials for the real thing up to a point, and I am only able to visualize the working and realization of an idea clearly if I am trying it out with the fabrics and threads I think I would like to use for the finished piece. Sometimes, for all sorts of reasons, the materials I envisaged using do not work as well as I had hoped, so then others have to be tried. These 'failures' are an essential part of the working process and record my personal growth and understanding of my subject matter and the materials and methods I am using. Very few people can succeed and obtain the best results at the first attempt and I have many examples that didn't quite work out, but I regard these as part of the 'story' of my progress towards finished work.

It has been said that risk in art is experimentation. By risking and embracing change we can develop growth in our work. Experiments, or sampling, with fabric and thread – maybe using a technique suggested by your subject matter, (as discussed above), a favourite method or, perhaps better still, trying a new one – allows more ideas to emmerge gradually and to show ways in which the subject might be expressed in terms of textiles. This process of discovery can be a slow one and it is important to give yourself the time to enjoy the whole journey and not to become discouraged if first attempts do not work to your complete satisfaction. Not only is it necessary to risk materials as we search for ways in which to express our ideas, but we have to be prepared to risk time, too – the time it takes to try things out that may not work. In my experience, 'playing safe' or 'staying in the comfort zone' may lead to acceptable work, but the really interesting developments occur, and I learn more, when I risk spending time on experiments that may either work well or may prove to be misjudged. I find that the search for materials, suitable techniques and ways of stitching as a means of interpreting ideas is always tricky but, nevertheless, is interesting and informative.

Reference to books and magazines giving sound information about stitches and techniques, is essential at the sampling stage of making work.

Above *Three Experimental Forms*. Hand-made
paper with fabric and stitching made over
moulds. See pages 88–93 for more on working
over a mould.

Right *Windows 1* by Jenny
Richardson (120 x 40cm).
A large hanging structure
based on reflections
observed in contemporary
architecture, illustrating
the use of mixed media for
practical as well as aesthetic
considerations. Tension is
maintained in the needle-
lace fillings in each module
by the heavy, fabric-covered
card frames.

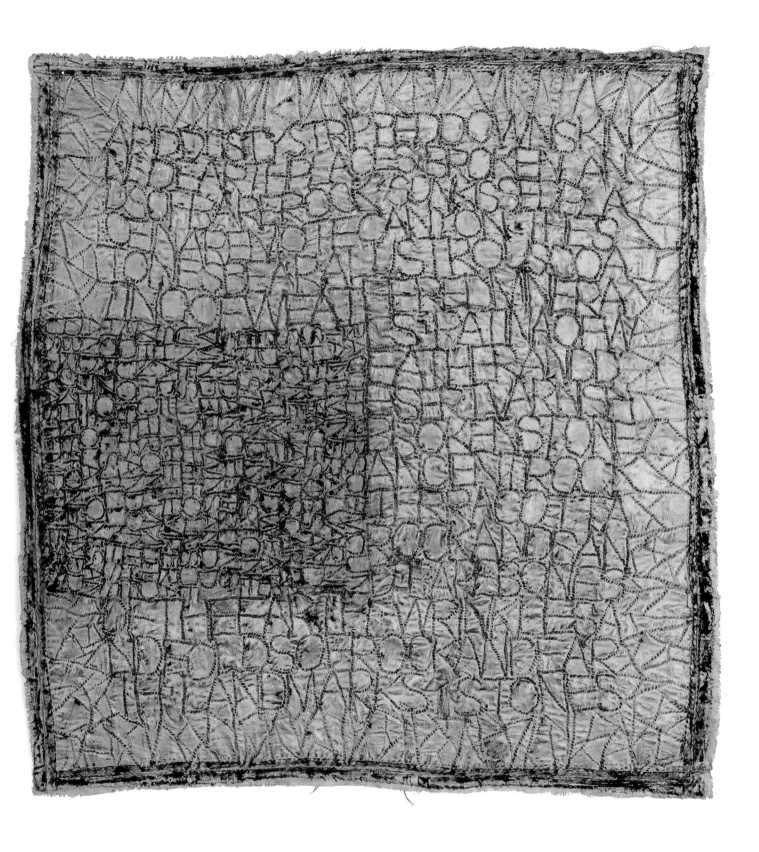

Above *Earth Quilt* (115 x 106cm). A dense pattern of text worked in raised whip stitch with a coating of clay slip and paint. The sanded clay refers to the colour of the landscape and the erosion of earth and rocks in the American southwest. See *Earth Quilt* detail on page 121.

PERSONAL INSPIRATIONS AND METHODS

Throughout my working life as a maker of stitched textiles, I would describe my own chosen method of stitching as structural. Even early in my career I always tried to make my stitching become part of the fabric, letting it gradually emerge from the background so that fabric, thread and stitch become integrated in the making of a whole new textured surface.

Gradually, in later work, as my design sources changed to the rugged rock formations and features of the desert landscapes in the American southwest, I felt the need for my stitching to echo more the dramatic structure of the areas that were so inspirational. I have described in Chapter 7 how influential some of the Indian tribal textiles have been in my embroidery and it was at this point that I was able, after much trial, error and sampling with different fabrics and threads, to evolve a way of working in which these different influences could come together. By putting very intense stitching under a great deal of tension, I eventually learned that I could physically thicken, manipulate and lift the fabric surface to completely change its character to one of exaggerated relief (see Developing Whip Stitch on page 119). More recently, this has slowly led to the making of completely three-dimensional stitched pieces, all being inspired by landscape and the peoples who inhabit it.

While many of the ideas shown in this book reflect my long-held interest in different aspects of landscape and have their origins in my frequent visits to particular and special places, both in the UK and abroad, the possibilities illustrated are by no means limited to this subject matter. There is huge potential for the adaptation of my methods to make many different types of work based on a range of themes.

The work shown in this book has all been developed according to the processes described in this chapter.

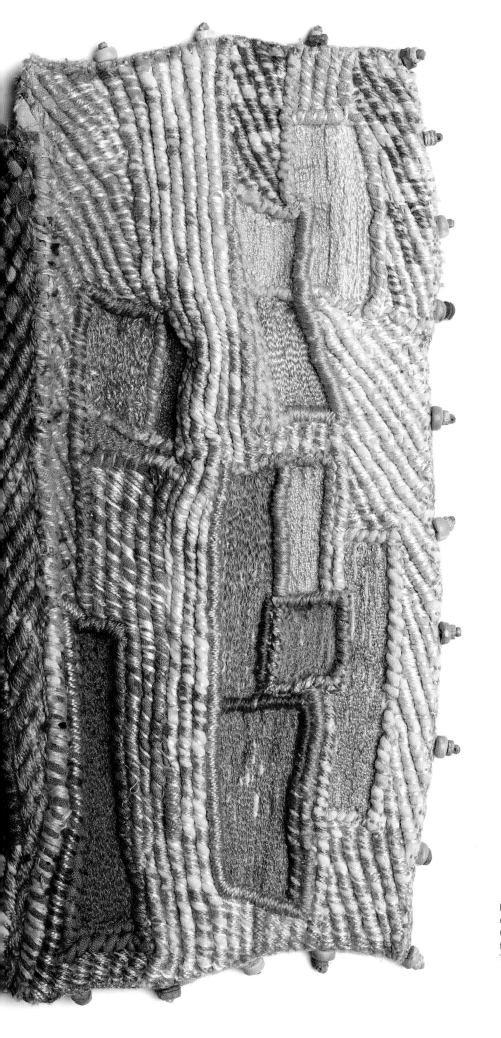

Left *Cliff Dwelling*. Detail of a small panel, based on rock dwellings, seen and drawn in Canyon de Chelly, USA. Whip stitch was used to manipulate the surface of the fabric into rugged textures. The flat areas are machine stitched.

MATERIALS

MIXED MEDIA

Throughout this book you will see that, alongside regular embroidery threads and fabrics, I have used a variety of other materials. I like to use natural materials such as canes, sticks and stems, as well as paint, paper, wax, wire and clay slip, but I only choose to use them where I think they are appropriate and enhance the idea of the piece. Mixed media, in my work, adds vital contrasts of shape, texture and visual weight and also emphasizes my reference to the natural world and to details of landscapes that I find so interesting. These materials, for me, are also symbolic of particular places and the peoples who inhabit them, for example *Earth Quilt* shown on page 27, and the use of horsehair in various work.

Other materials used with stitch do not only provide visual interest but can be helpful in providing tension, definition and additional strength to a piece of work. In some instances, it is appropriate to disguise the strengthening material so that its presence is for practical purposes only rather than being a prominent design feature.

If you would like to introduce other materials and use them alongside your regular textile ones, it is a good idea to visit exhibitions and look at books and catalogues showing the work of artists exploring ideas in other fine art and craft disciplines, where there is a great deal of exciting and inspiring work to be seen.

Below *Two Spiky Forms* (height 13cm and 24cm). Wrapped sticks, horsehair, thread and fabric supported on bases made from polystyrene spheres.

FURTHER WORK: YOU COULD...

Begin a collection of information to stimulate ideas for your stitched textiles.

Become more observant in order to discover and understand how things around you are constructed. Look for examples of interesting structure in your home, in your garden, when you go for a walk, when you travel and, also, in books.

Refer to the lists of possible sources of organic and man-made structures given on pages 12 and 15 and focus on those subjects that hold most appeal for you. With the help of a magnifying glass, if necessary, begin to look at surface (exterior) and more hidden structures.

Record the different types of structure you find in terms of brief notes, photographs, diagrams and drawings. If what you see reminds you of a particular stitch, textile technique or material, make a brief note of this and, if necessary, a note to remind you to refresh your knowledge of a certain method.

The following check points and questions could be helpful as you are looking and drawing, making notes and taking photographs. Look for and record:

- Linear construction and the lines you see. Are they thin, thick, smooth, textured, curved or straight? How are the lines organized: parallel, criss-cross, some other form? Are they gentle and soft or sharp, tense and dynamic?
- How the lines join each other, or how they connect to solid shapes. What types of angle do they produce?
- The shapes between the lines (the negative shapes). What type of shape do you see?
- Other shapes. What are their characteristics – organic and curved, geometric and angular? Does one shape dominate or repeat?
- The way you think structural strength is achieved within your subject.
- Other features, such as rhythms, patterns and textures. How could you translate these?

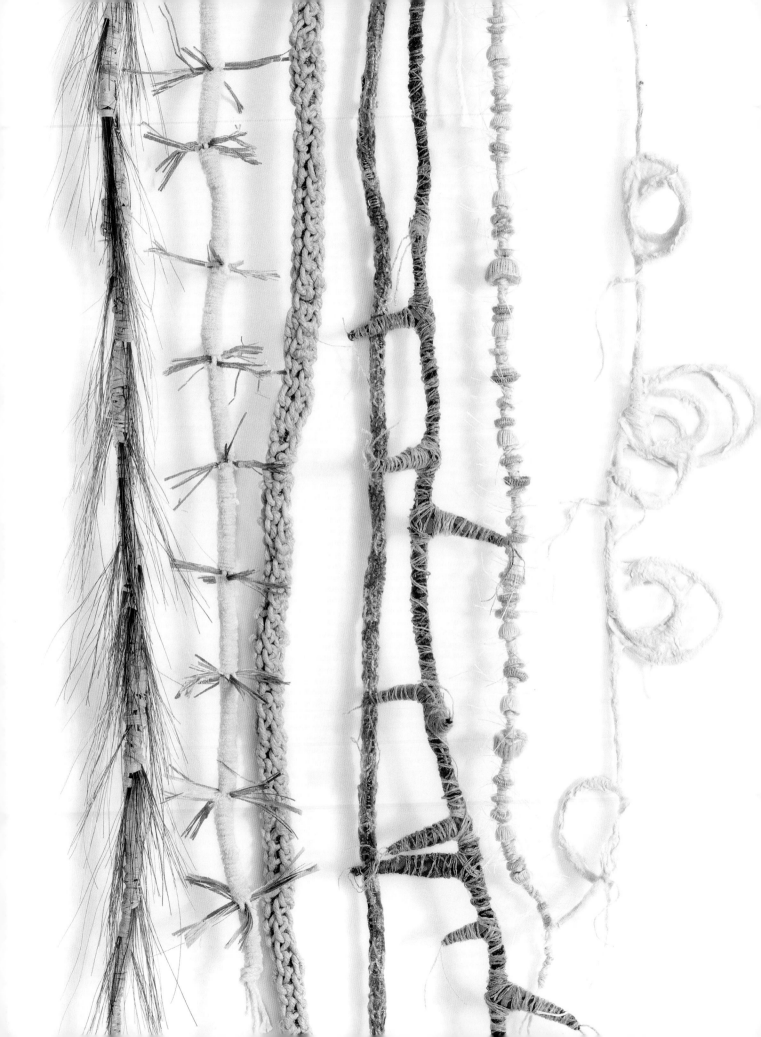

MORE THAN
THREAD

Pushing the boundaries with threads.
Experimenting and making unusual threads.
Thinking of thread as a linear structure.

Opposite Linear structures made from various
materials including horsehair; synthetic sinew
and natural raffia; ruched knitting ribbon;
spikes of raw hemp; buttonhole stitch in fine
string; bound points (see page 106 for method)
bound onto a cord with natural raffia; wire; tiny
buttonhole-stitched rings; looped thread dipped
in paper pulp. The third and fourth examples
from the left were made by Val Brewin.

Mark Siegeltuch has pointed out in his book *The Thread Spirit: the Symbolism of Knotting and the Fiber Arts* that, throughout history and in many different cultures, not only has thread had practical uses, but it has also held a deeply symbolic significance, often representing destiny and the continuation of life.

In Hinduism, for example, thread is the connector of this world and the afterlife. Some Hindu groups participate in a coming-of-age ceremony during which a sacred thread is presented and worn. In the Neolithic period there was a widespread distribution of knot technologies for record keeping and measurement. In Western cultures, thread has been regarded as so important and central to life, because of the importance of textiles, that terms connected with it and its making have entered the language and are still in common use in other contexts. Just one example of this is when we say that we are afraid of 'losing the thread'.

In stitched textiles, thread is the basic stuff of all that we do and the materials we use. Fabrics of all kinds, whether they are woven or knitted, interlaced, etc., are constructed from it and, of course, we use thread to stitch with – both in practical sewing and for embellishment. The linear quality of thread in all its varieties, together with the large repertoire of stitches available, provides us with huge scope for using line in an interesting manner in all forms of embroidery. Therefore, alongside gathering information, as described in the last chapter, consideration of thread is a good place to begin investigating structure in terms of stitched textiles.

Today, besides conventional, familiar embroidery threads, we are very fortunate in having many other exciting ones to choose from. Most people are aware of the wonderful array of knitting yarns now available, but it is also worth looking out for other unusual threads

Left and right Linear structures made by transforming conventional embroidery threads, or by using them in greater quantities than normal. Various forms of wrapping, knotting, multiple knotting and over stitching were used. The two examples on the far right were made by the Casalguidi method.

and fibres. Less rigid boundaries between previously discrete craft disciplines, together with the increasing use of mixed media in stitched textiles, have brought to light interesting threads and yarns, both from other countries and different craft processes. These may be new to us or may not be ones that we have considered using before. Some suppliers are now offering threads in a variety of thicknesses and textures made from paper, hemp, sisal, ramie, linen, pineapple, nettles and a variety of raw silks. In addition, DIY stores and other non-conventional places for finding embroidery materials are excellent sources for strings, cords, ropes, plastics, foam, nylon, wire and various kinds of tubing. While many of these cannot be threaded in a needle or used in the customary manner, all these linear materials have potential for use as more adventurous 'threads'. Sometimes, the ways in which these more unusual substances are wound, reeled and twisted in hanks, skeins and balls make them structurally interesting in themselves.

The direction that my work has gradually taken, due to my increasing interest in particular sources of inspiration, has meant that I have needed to search for, and use, different kinds of threads. Strangely, these more unusual threads have, in turn, influenced and accelerated changes in what I can achieve. In addition, some of the natural plant-fibre threads have an organic, rough quality that seems totally suited to my land-based subject matter. I now have a considerable collection of threads made from a variety of natural and man-made materials.

The purpose of this chapter is to explore what threads can be. If, instead of thinking of thread as a sewing material only, we begin to develop the idea of thread as a more complex and decorative linear structure, unhampered by flexibility, size and practicality, very exciting possibilities for using it in very creative ways start to emerge.

CONVENTIONAL THREADS

While many people have favourite threads, it is very easy to get into a rut and perhaps no longer use even the full range of embroidery threads available. Sadly some threads tend to go out of fashion and their usefulness becomes forgotten. A good exercise is to re-visit your store of threads to see if you have some forgotten or neglected ones. Do some appear 'old fashioned' and unsuitable for use in contemporary work? Can you rethink their use by altering them in some way – by re-inventing them?

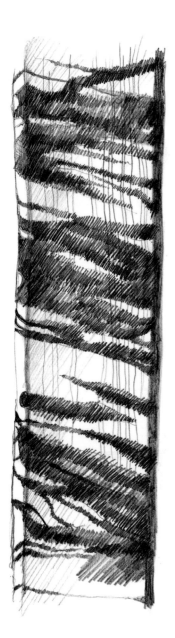

ALTERING CONVENTIONAL THREADS AND INVENTING NEW ONES

While it is possible to use almost any threads you already own, you may find that some of them, particularly the softer, fluffy ones, if used alone or unaltered, lack enough body to enable you to make firm or visually strong structures. In order to explore their new creative potential, as described opposite, for old or conventional threads, it is necessary to use them liberally and in greater quantities than you are used to. In asking you to experiment, you may feel that I am suggesting you squander thread but, then, if you put the exciting threads you make to good use, nothing will be wasted. You will find that you will be able to use your newly structured threads in some of the ideas suggested in later chapters of this book.

Left Drawing of shadows on a garden post suggesting wrapped threads.

Right Drawings of desert plants and stems as inspiration for linear structures.

In order to transform threads and give them new life, you could try some of the following ideas:

- tie several threads together in bundles to make thicker, more substantial ones
- knot and loop threads to alter their appearance
- twist many threads together to make much thicker cords
- ruche a plied thread or a handmade cord to create an uneven texture
- wrap threads by hand or machine stitching – singly or in multiples
- combine wire or a stronger thread (for example, string) with conventional threads
- stiffen threads with dilute PVA, paint or hot or acrylic wax for extra body.

You will find that if you experiment freely, initially without thought for practicality, you will achieve very imaginative and exciting results.

At this point, if you have not already done so, you could try working with harder, larger-scale, less conventional threads, for example, heavy linens and knitting yarns, hemp, raffia, paper threads, plastics and wire. You could also incorporate other materials such as fabric strips, leather thongs, sticks and beads to create your own exciting and unique thread structures.

Reference to the notes and diagrams you made when looking for structure should be helpful. Interesting linear structures, such as stems, branches and skeletal forms, could be used as inspirational starting points.

Right Detail of a hanging made from a group of linear structures. Cords wrapped with hemp, raffia and synthetic sinew and knotted with silk-paper threads.

Right Long hanging
structure made from
loosely wrapped
paper threads which
were knotted and
looped, then dipped
in paper pulp.

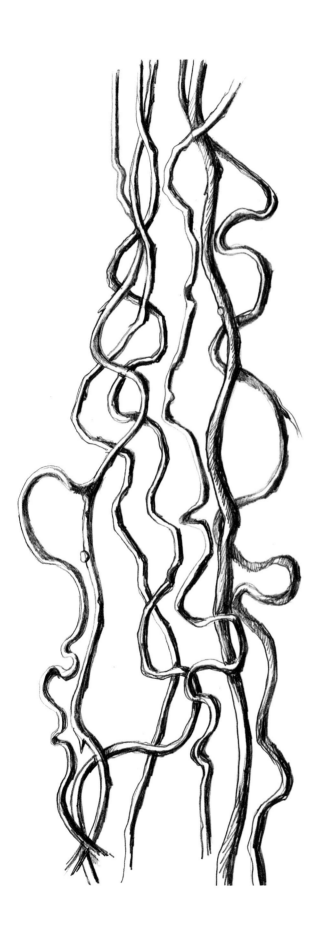

FURTHER WORK: YOU COULD...

Select the most successful experimental linear structures you have made and now create longer lengths to be used in future work, possibly in some of the structures suggested in the next chapter.

While retaining the energy and lively quality of your experimental samples, spend time refining and making your linear structures well crafted. They need to be beautiful enough to justify the time you will take in using them in the development of more resolved pieces of work.

Left Drawing of weeping twisted wilow branches as inspiration for linear structures opposite.

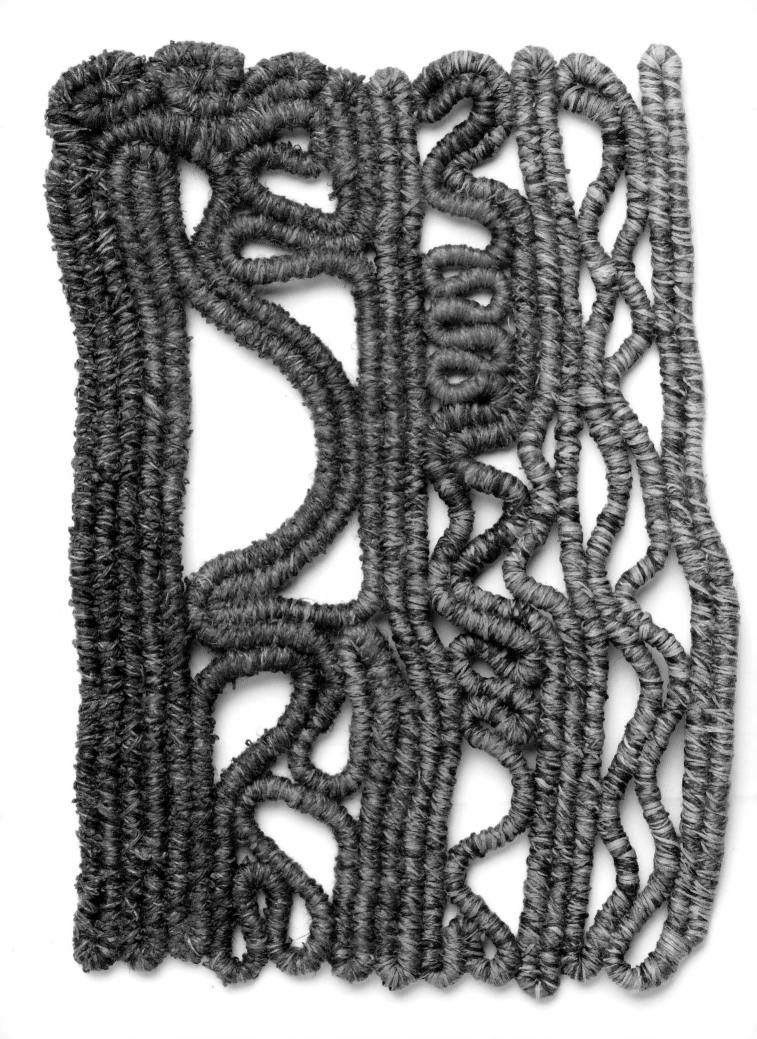

CONSTRUCTING WITH THREADS AND LINEAR STRUCTURES

Extending the line. Exploring the use of bold threads and linear structures in the making of two- and three-dimensional work.

Opposite A flat coiled structure made with a core cord that was freely wrapped with various threads before coiling began. For the construction method see diagrams on pages 50–51. As in the small pods on page 47, the construction stitches are spaced to allow the core cord to show.

Left A heavy mixed bunch of conventional embroidery threads were knotted and over-knotted several times, making a very uneven, textured linear structure, as illustrated on page 34. This was arranged on adhesive soluble fabric and stitched as described in Chapter 5. The turquoise loops were added later.

Right An intuitively constructed sculptural form made from one of the linear structures illustrated on page 32. Wrapped heavy wire with bound points, see page 106 for method.

EXPERIMENTING WITH THREAD AS LINE

There are many interesting and imaginative ways in which to use your decorative handmade threads – and purchased threads – in order to make a wide variety of relief, hanging and three-dimensional structures. The emphasis in this chapter is on the linear elements – the threads themselves. These are the prominent features in the work and any other stitching used is supplementary or only for practical, constructional reasons.

If you make enough of any of your threads, you will find that, in placing them together in close multiple lines, the impact they make is greatly increased. By simply hanging long threads together, possibly from a rod, very dynamic hanging structures could be made.

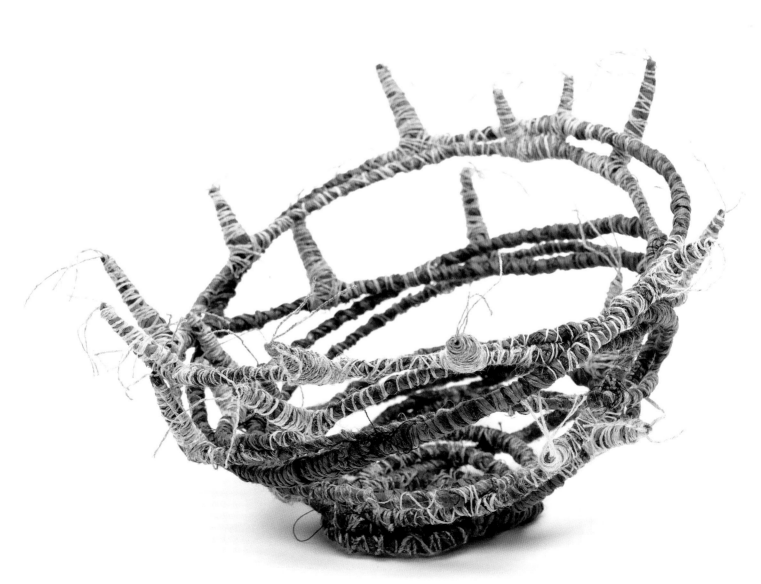

Perhaps the most immediate and obvious way to use the exciting threads you make would be to couch them on to a background fabric to make a highly textured structured surface. The new surface would appear more intense if the threads were laid close together, or the background fabric was partially cut away.

Depending on the characteristics of the line or element, you can readily begin to try out other arrangements and forms that do not rely on being set on a fabric background. By experimenting with the elements you have made, manipulating and grouping them together,

interesting structural ideas will emerge. Some applications may need the support of a temporary stabilizer or a mould to hold the threads in position while you are assembling the piece (see page 88). If your threads do not have enough 'body' to support the structure you have made, the finished work could be stiffened with dilute PVA.

The experimental and the more resolved forms illustrated here are made with a variety of my threads.

Opposite above
An experimental
three-dimensional
form, made from
wrapped cords (left),
was intuitively shaped,
twisted and stitched
into place. The starting
point was a long narrow
strip constructed from
square modules
similar to the one
shown (right).

Opposite left
Experimental form
constructed from
a number of short
forked threads, slotted
together. These were
made from bunches
of silk paper fibres,
wrapped with natural,
heavy hemp thread.

Right Trailing
experimental form
made from doubled
heavy cords, unevenly
wrapped with hemp,
synthetic sinew
and natural raffia.
Unstructured tassels
were made from
horsehair. The
looped, upper part
of the structure was
made by intuitively
twisting and stitching
the cords together.

FURTHER WORK: YOU COULD...

Consider and experiment with arrangements of your linear elements, such as:

Solid surfaces; open, lacy surfaces; grids and weaves; random crossing of lines; hanging structures; knotted forms; stacks.

Any of the above could be secured by stitching.

Left Detail of the piece shown on page 40. Notice how the core thread was allowed to show under the wrapping stitches, creating a mottled appearance.

COILED FORMS

Despite having been put off cane basketry many years ago by some of the rather conventional work I saw being made at that time, I have always collected small baskets from around the world. Books and exhibitions featuring the work of contemporary basket makers, who use a variety of materials to make innovative work, have inspired me and opened my eyes to interesting possibilities. Having learned that it is thought that some of the first embroidery stitches developed from early baskets, I asked a friend to teach me how to make coiled forms. Much of my three-dimensional work has grown out of that informal lesson.

Coiling is an ancient and culturally widespread technique used for the making of baskets as well as flat shapes used for mats, decorative screens, etc. Essentially it consists of some kind of substantial, but flexible, core or foundation, which is gradually wrapped with a finer thread as construction proceeds, in a spiralling fashion, from a central starting point. Each wrapped line is attached to the preceding one by frequently passing the wrapping thread around the row below, so forming a very firm structure.

Above *Pods* by Margaret Raine. A group of small, very finely coiled forms made in the hand. The fine silk core thread was allowed to show between the spaced wrapping stitches which were made from one strand of stranded cotton Bronze seed beads decorate the top edges.

Coiled baskets are often made from plant materials that are readily available in the makers' environment. The core is usually composed of a bunch of stems or grasses that are then wrapped with a single, thinner one. Fine examples can be seen in the work of the indigenous peoples of Australia and some of the Native American tribes, as well as many other cultures. The materials used and the forms and decoration favoured varies according to the customs and traditions of the makers. The method is by no means restricted to the use of plant material – many types of thread, yarn, string and rope can also be used in conjunction with other materials.

Above and opposite *OzDots* (ranging in size from 6cm to 12cm). Details of a large installation of 200 coiled forms, symbolizing the vibrant colours of Australian plants, birds and the baskets made by the indigenous people. Wool, silk and cotton with mixed media decoration.

METHOD: COILING

REQUIREMENTS:
- A long core or foundation thread (e.g. heavy string, cord or thin rope such as washing line)
- Wrapping thread (e.g. wool, linen, stranded cotton, cotton perle or other)
- A tapestry needle

1. Make a loop at the end of the foundation thread. If a thick thread is being used, the bulk can be reduced and controlled by fraying the end and cutting away some of the strands.

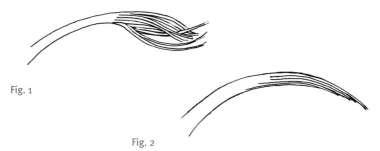

Fig. 1

Fig. 2

2. With the outside or wrapping thread, wrap the end of the foundation thread, starting near the loop (fig. 3), then pass the needle and thread through the loop and pull tightly to form the work into a circle (fig. 4). There will be a small hole in the centre. The length of this initial wrapping will depend upon the thickness of the core and how readily it can be formed into a circle.

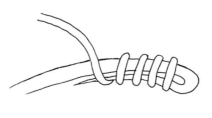

Fig. 3

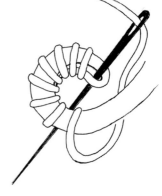

3. Proceed to guide the foundation around the centre gradually, holding it in place with wrapping stitches, each of which passes through the central hole (fig. 5).

Fig. 4

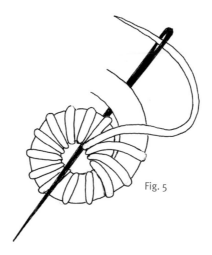

Fig. 5

4. When one round has been completed and you have reached the loop once more, work then proceeds on individual foundation rows wrapping two or three times round the outside foundation thread, then stitching a figure of eight stitch into the preceding row (fig. 6)

Fig. 6

5. All ending and joining threads are laid along the foundation thread and wrapped into the work invisibly.

6. It is usual to coil a flat disc for a base first before beginning to shape the sides of the form.

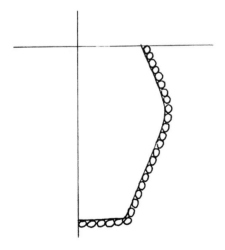

Fig. 7

7. The form can be shaped gradually to be wide or narrow by careful placement of the foundation thread (slightly outwards or inwards in relation to the previous row) as spiralling progresses. Fig. 7 shows how one side of a form might be shaped.

8. The form is finished by carefully reducing the thickness of the foundation thread as was done at the start so that the ends can be wrapped in with the preceding row. Darn in the end of the thread.

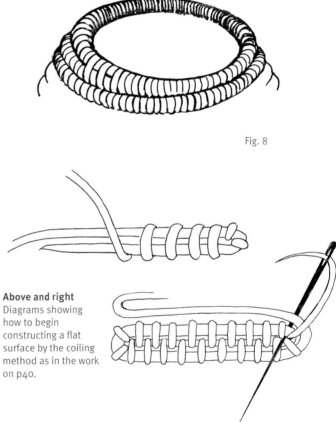

Fig. 8

Above and right
Diagrams showing how to begin constructing a flat surface by the coiling method as in the work on p40.

Primarily, coiling produces a circular or oval form, but asymmetrical, sculptural forms can also be built, as can flat, asymmetrical designs (see page 40 for an example).

The method described is the basic one I use, but there are many others, producing different patterns and finishes. For first-time practice, wool used as a wrapping thread is a good, forgiving choice, as the stitches blend well, giving a smooth result.

As with many methods, repetition of a form, using one shape as a module, adds to the visual strength of a piece of work or installation.

Above *Coiled Forms* by
Barbara Meeke. A group
of very small forms coiled
with hemp over a heavy
cord. The top edges are
coiled in a rhythmic,
free-form manner.
Clustered together they
make an interesting relief
construction for a wall.

In her use of hemp in neutral tones, which show up the light and dark areas of the work, thereby emphasizing the forms, Barbara Meeke has created a group of small coiled baskets. Placed together, these little baskets combine to produce an interesting relief structure.

By contrast, my large installation *OzDots* (see pages 48–49), comprising of 200 brightly coloured coiled baskets relies on the effect created by the vivid colours seen side by side and on the mixed-media decoration on the edges of some of the forms. Because I changed the colour of the wrapping threads frequently, the linear character of the coiling technique is very prominent. I found the making of this display was exciting because I could not predict how the colours would look together as the coiling progressed. Considerable colour blending occurred when the thread being used encroached into the previous colour in the figure of eight stitch of the process. The materials used in this display are largely wool threads with some silk and cotton ones, too, wrapped over cords and thick string. The inspiration was my reaction to the intense colours of the Australian landscape, its flowers and birds, and the brightly coloured, plant-dyed baskets made by some Australian Aboriginal people.

Right A finely coiled basket made from a visible core of polished hemp from Indonesia, stitched with black machine thread. The top edge is decorated with a linear structure made from spikes of synthetic sinew and small ceramic beads.

Above Two coiled baskets made by the method described opposite. Long lengths of the core or foundation thread were first wrapped in strips of fabric before being constructed, in a spiral manner, with stitching. On the left: buttonhole stitch. On the right: additional uneven wrapping with fine threads then joined with long stitches around the cord and into the fabric of the previous row.

Above left Basket form made with stitched and coiled kozo fibre.

Above right Delicate lacy basket form made with intuitively looped and coiled fine wire and silk thread. Note the closely coiled base contrasting with the open sides.

An alternative method of coiling to that described on pages 50–51 would be to first wrap the foundation thread, along its length, with narrow strips of fabric. Then, beginning from the centre and, again working in a spiral manner, stitch the form together. This could be done invisibly using ordinary sewing thread, or the joining stitches could show and add decoration to the work. This method, in conjunction with a less formal working of the basic method previously described, would also be suitable if you wished to make a form from one of your decorative linear elements.

Once the method is understood, free, more experimental forms with undulations, spaces and extensions can be undertaken, as in the examples shown below left. The more delicate piece was made from fine wire wrapped in silk thread, allowing for a very open, lacy surface. The other white example, made from beaten bark fibres from the Kozo plant (a type of mulberry tree), was partly wrapped and partly stitched with silk thread. Kozo has enough body to hold a form if stitched and wrapped carefully.

FURTHER STUDY: YOU COULD...

Look up and practise other methods of basket construction.

Experiment with forms made from your own threads.

Try using a range of different materials for the core thread, from clothes line and rope to dried grasses or wire.

Consider using handspun yarns for the core or wrapping threads.

Try constructing more adventurous flat and three-dimensional forms.

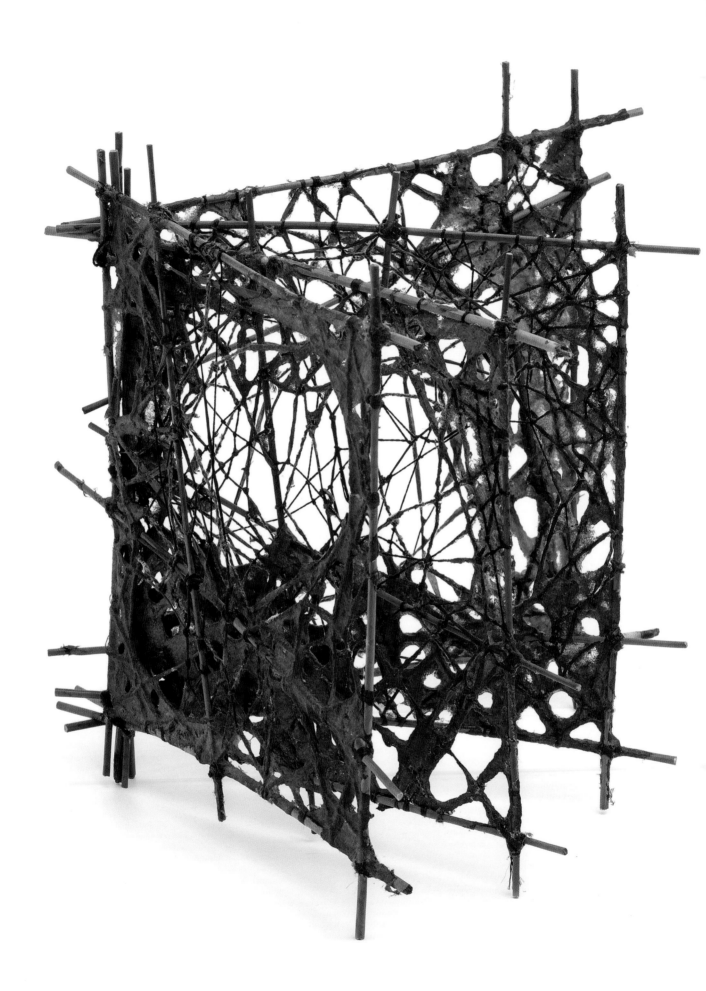

STITCHES IN THIN AIR

Using soluble fabric for fragile, hand-stitched structured surfaces and as a stabilizer for constructed work.

Opposite *Book Form* (height 18cm) Four modules were made with thin sticks mounted on non-adhesive soluble fabric as support. They were stitched with random, knotted needle-lace stitches (see p63) in fine black cotton perle thread, then dipped in black paper pulp. The modules were stitched together at the 'spine'.

When we think of stitching, our usual starting point is to reach for a piece of fabric so that we can work stitches upon it. This and the following chapter are concerned with increasing understanding of the imaginative and creative potential of structures made from stitch alone, without the need for a conventional background fabric. This is a method that I find increasingly useful. When fabric is omitted, the form, rhythm and lacy surface structures created by the thread and stitch alone become distinct and very striking. As shown in this chapter, work made in this manner can be immensely delicate and fragile, or extremely bold and robust.

The very large piece shown here, measuring 152 x 62cm (60 x 24in), is by Susan Walker. It is made from rough slivers of slate, very heavy cotton perle thread and soluble fabric. Susan's method of working was to trap the slate pieces between two layers of thick soluble fabric, binding them in place with large horizontal hand stitches that passed around them. Working from top to bottom, the next stage was to create a grid of twisted chain stitch, linking all the pieces together. When the soluble fabric was dissolved, the slate pieces were left secure in a net-like structure of stitches. This heavy work hangs on a metal rod.

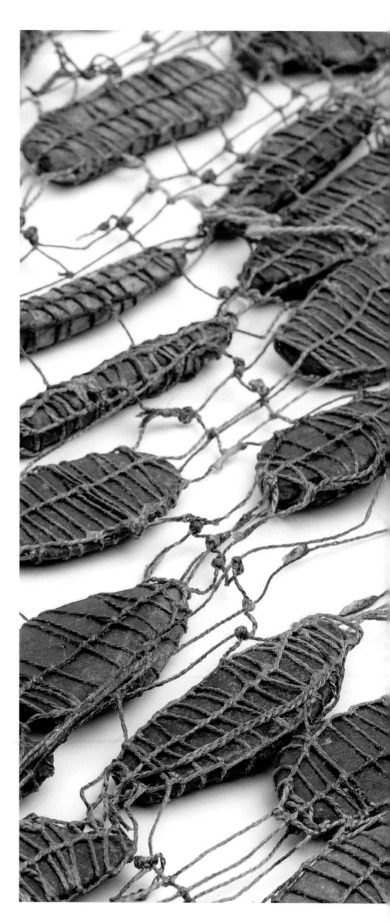

Right *Dovey Reflections* (detail) by Susan Walker. Large stitched hanging with suspended slate as described above.

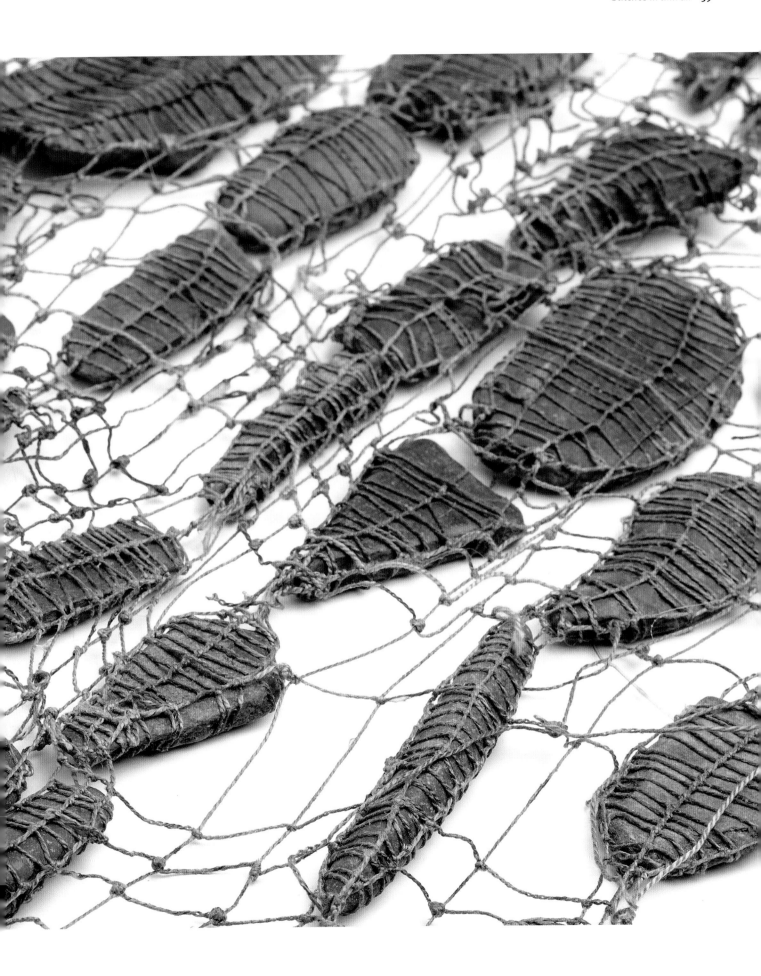

SOLUBLE FABRICS FOR HAND STITCHING

Soluble fabrics, available in various forms and weights, have been widely used for many years, mainly by machine embroiderers in the making of fragile lacy surfaces, which are then often applied to a background fabric. In the context of structured textiles, this machine-stitched technique could bear rethinking, possibly alone, or in conjunction with some of the mixed media shown in this book, without the need for the usual support of a background fabric. The versatility and many virtues and uses of these stabilizers have been described and demonstrated by other authors and artists, so I do not propose to repeat basic machine techniques here. Instead, my primary concern is the perhaps less well-known use of soluble fabrics as a basis for stitching by hand; a method I have used extensively over a period of time. All the work shown in this chapter has been hand stitched on soluble fabric.

While the white opaque variety of non-adhesive soluble fabric is pleasant to handle because it feels soft and much more like regular fabric, I find the transparent kind is much easier to use for hand stitching as both sides of the work can be readily seen while stitching is in progress. With a little persistence and practice one gets used to the plastic surface, and I find the interesting results make coping with the somewhat strange feel of the soluble fabric worthwhile. I usually put my soluble fabric in a frame so that I am actually handling it as little as possible and also to enable me to control the tension of the stitching.

Not all hand stitches are suitable for working on soluble fabric and care has to be taken both with the choice of stitch and its execution. From the onset it has to be remembered that there will be no real back to the work, so the totality of thread forming the stitch, including fastening on and off, will be revealed when the fabric is dissolved. Perhaps this could be described as uncovering the whole structure, the anatomy, of the stitch. By choosing your stitches wisely and by employing a few basic techniques, both delicate and robust lacy structures can be constructed from hand stitching.

Stitches that lend themselves to this method include: running stitch (producing a line of thread); Cretan stitch; knotted Cretan stitch; buttonhole stitch; herringbone stitch; needle weaving; some forms of couching, and some of the stitches worked on a linear base, such as woven wheels.

As you experiment with stitching on soluble fabric, you will quickly see how the linking of stitches is essential if the work is to hold together. You will find your own inventive ways of doing this and, so long as your work is well crafted, it does not matter if your stitches are no longer 'by the book'.

In Chapter 2, I discuss my views on the necessity of taking risks with materials and time in order to develop new working ideas. Along with many others shown, this set of samples exemplifies this approach. Making them took a great deal of time and patience, yet I did not know, until the soluble fabric was removed, if they would successfully connect to make reliable surfaces.

Cohesion and safe linking of surface is achieved, in the examples shown, by employing some of the following techniques:

- Connecting stitches, overlapping and criss-crossing lines of stitches
- Piercing or splitting with the needle the thread of previously worked lines of stitches as successive lines are worked
- Working knots around an already worked line as a new one crosses it
- Working many layers of stitches, perhaps fragile ones, to give more substance and body to the work
- Using some form of grid, possibly machined with invisible thread, to support hand stitching (once the fabric has been dissolved and dried, unwanted visible parts of the grid can be cut away)
- Trapping other threads, fibres or snippets of fabric between two thin layers of soluble fabric before stitching, to give additional body and texture to the work (see page 98)
- Adding other materials, (e.g. sticks or wires) to create tension, greater stability and contrast. Several examples are shown on pages 68–71.

The hand-stitched samples, shown on pages 62–67, were worked on thin, non-adhesive soluble fabric. These were formed in the ways shown in the following diagrams and captions.

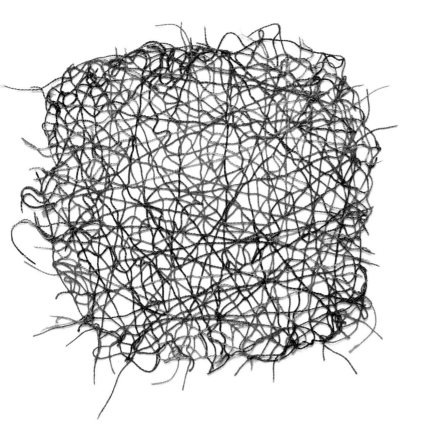

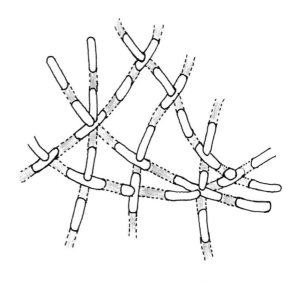

Left Many rows of running stitch were worked randomly right across the soluble fabric. At each crossing, the bottom thread was pierced with the needle as a new row was worked (see diagram below). Cotton perle thread was used throughout.

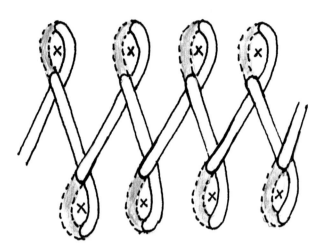

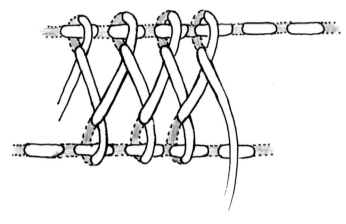

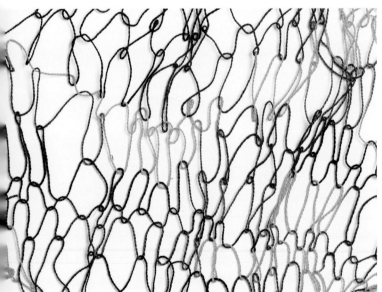

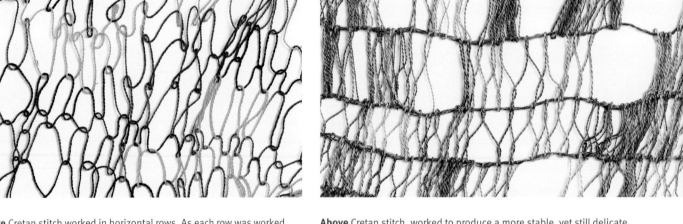

Above Cretan stitch worked in horizontal rows. As each row was worked, care was taken to connect the new stitches into the ends of stitches in the previous row at X (see diagram, top). This produced a very open structure where the twist on the stitches is not always maintained. Space-dyed cotton perle thread was used.

Above Cretan stitch, worked to produce a more stable, yet still delicate, structure. Horizontal rows of running stitch were worked first to act as an anchor for the Cretan stitch. Care was taken to loop the thread around the running stitch in the working of the blocks of Cretan stitch. Space-dyed cotton perle thread was used here.

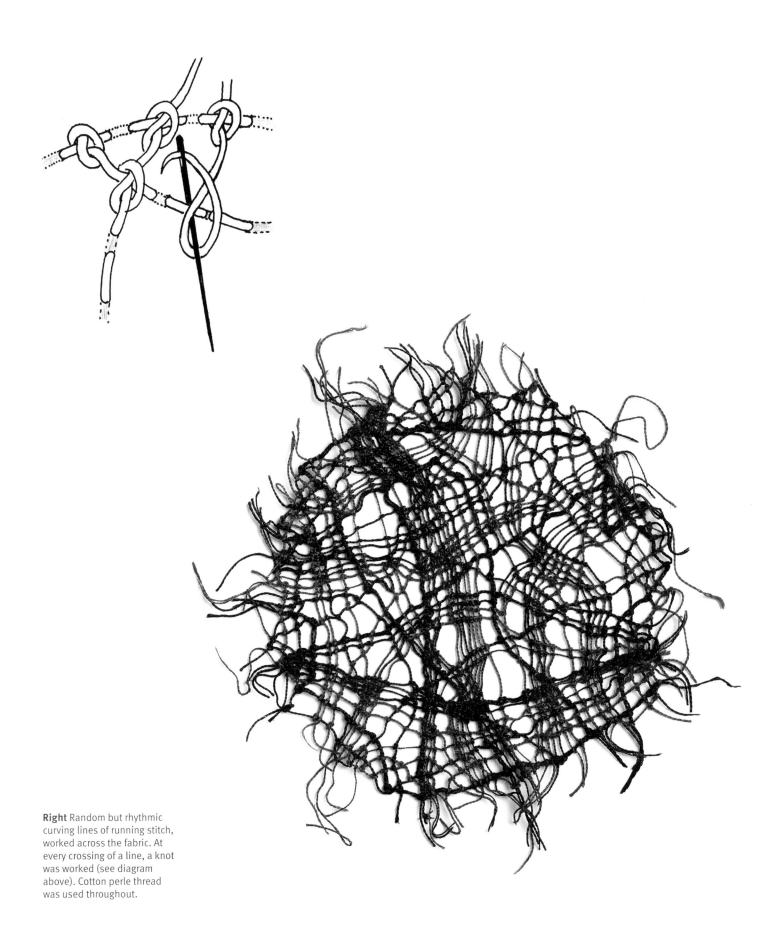

Right Random but rhythmic curving lines of running stitch, worked across the fabric. At every crossing of a line, a knot was worked (see diagram above). Cotton perle thread was used throughout.

Right Begun in the same manner as the sample on page 63, more prominent knots were produced by working double knot stitch over the bottom thread at each intersection (see diagrams above). Some of the stitch rows were worked closely to produce contrast within the linear structure. Worked in cotton perle and heavier soft cotton thread.

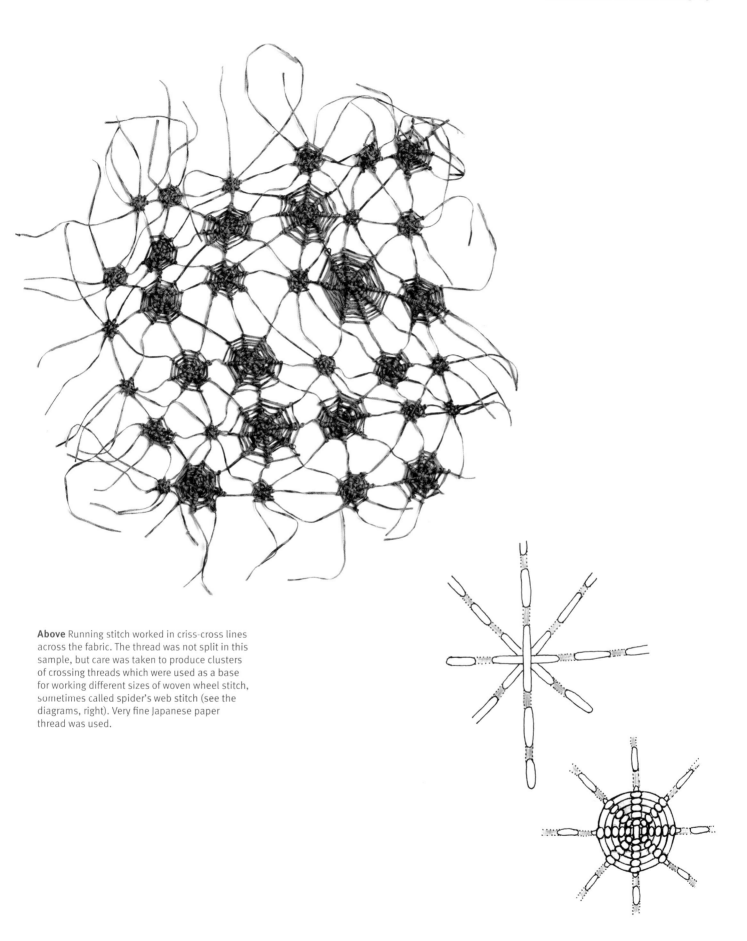

Above Running stitch worked in criss-cross lines across the fabric. The thread was not split in this sample, but care was taken to produce clusters of crossing threads which were used as a base for working different sizes of woven wheel stitch, sometimes called spider's web stitch (see the diagrams, right). Very fine Japanese paper thread was used.

Above Fragments of soft silk threads were trapped between two layers of thin soluble fabric. Uneven, but fine, Cretan stitch was worked randomly in layers all over the work (see the diagram, right). The stitches are caught and held in place by the silk fragments, enabling the surface to hold together when the soluble fabric was dissolved. Produced using silk thread fragments and stitching in one strand of stranded cotton.

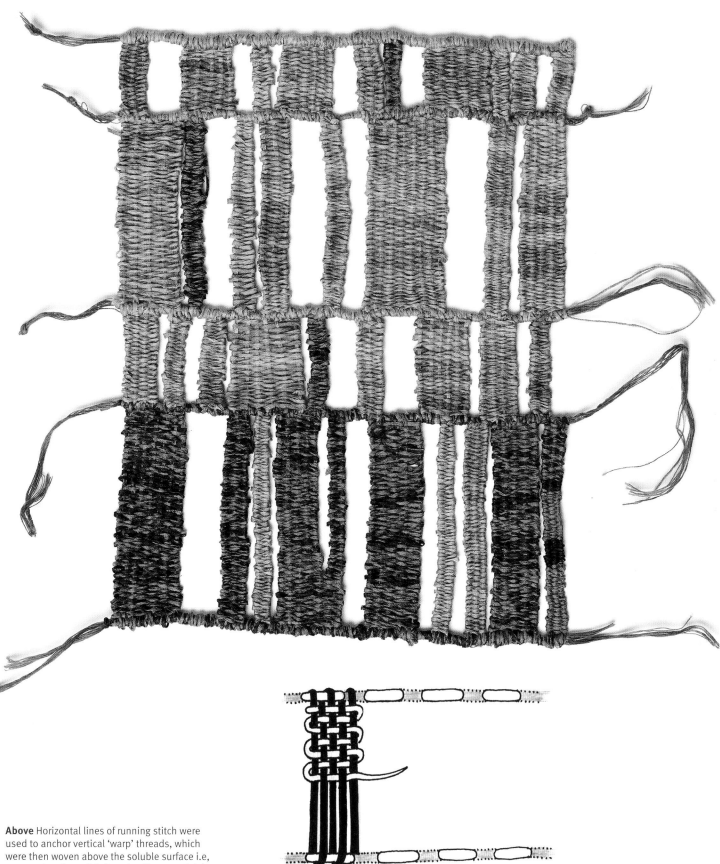

Above Horizontal lines of running stitch were used to anchor vertical 'warp' threads, which were then woven above the soluble surface i.e, not passing through it (see the diagram, right). Two types of Japanese paper thread were used.

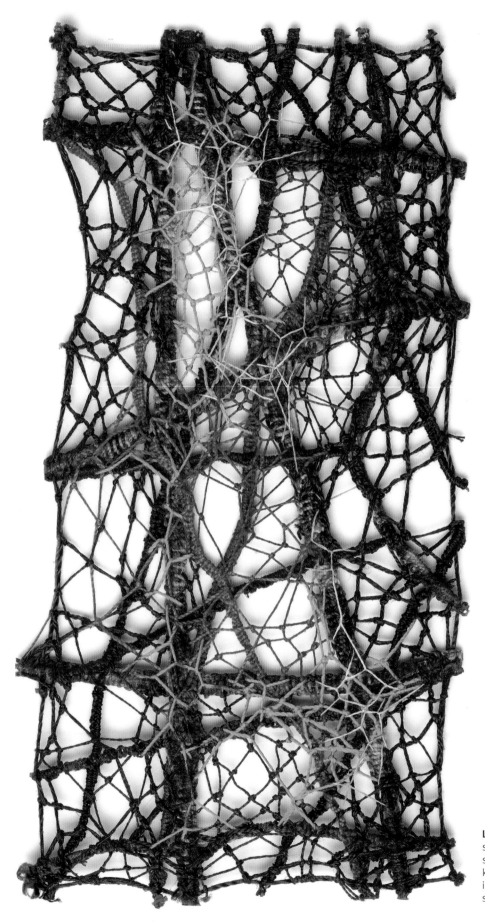

Left Wires were covered in close buttonhole stitch then trapped between two layers of thin soluble fabric. Layers of asymmetrically placed knotted stitches (see page 63) were worked in fine threads across and between the wire structure, maintaining the stitch tension.

Above A delicate, flexible structure made by trapping teased-out fine silk fibres and white sticks between two layers of transparent soluble fabric. Long rows of meandering running stitch, in fine silk thread, were worked the length of the piece, taking care to wrap the thread around each stick as it was reached. The piece shown on page 127 was worked in a similar manner.

While many different threads can be used for this method, wool, because of its springy nature, may prove troublesome.

When stitching is complete and the rinsing stage is reached, fragile, fine structures must be supported in a sieve or on a fine wire mesh as they are held under a running tap. This method prevents damage and tangles occurring. Drain the work and dry it on paper towels.

The samples described above show fragile stitch structures that could be used in a number of ways. Two examples, on pages 68–69, show how fragile surfaces can be supported with the help of wire, sticks and other mixed media. In other examples, different materials were trapped between two layers of thin soluble fabric before construction stitching was begun. But there are also possibilities for layering well-chosen fragile structures one above another as well as using them as a fragile background behind intricately worked motifs.

The extent to which the soluble residue is removed from the stitching is a matter of choice: very thorough washing results in a soft, pliable structure but, if a stiffer finish is required, some of the solution may be left behind. If residue is left in the stitched structure, at the wet stage it could be draped or manipulated over another form to give a raised shape when dry.

The small book form, shown on page 56 and below, and the large construction opposite, both with paper pulp as part of the structure, are examples of different outcomes from similar starting points. These were made as follows:

Square-shaped modules were individually made using soluble fabric, in a small frame, as a stabilizer. A framework of thin sticks was assembled, the corners being firmly stitched through the soluble fabric. Perle thread was used to stitch in a random criss-cross manner, between the sticks. The threads were knotted at each intersection and care was taken to ensure the tension on the threads was maintained throughout. When stitching was complete, all the squares were individually rinsed to dissolve the soluble fabric, then dried on paper towels.

At this point, the squares that make up the book form were dipped in black paper pulp, see the description in the caption below. Those intended for the large construction opposite were re-assembled on a fresh piece of soluble fabric. They were stitched in place where the sticks overlapped and more stitching (wrapped bars) was added in some of the spaces. The work was then completed as described in the caption to the piece.

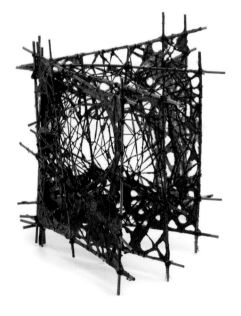

Left *Book Form.* Once the individual squares for this had been stitched as described above, a thin black paper pulp was made and the squares were individually dipped by tilting them to ensure all the stitching was not obscured. When dry, the squares were stitched together to resemble a book, so that an overlapping of the lacy surfaces was obtained. Other arrangements could have been used.

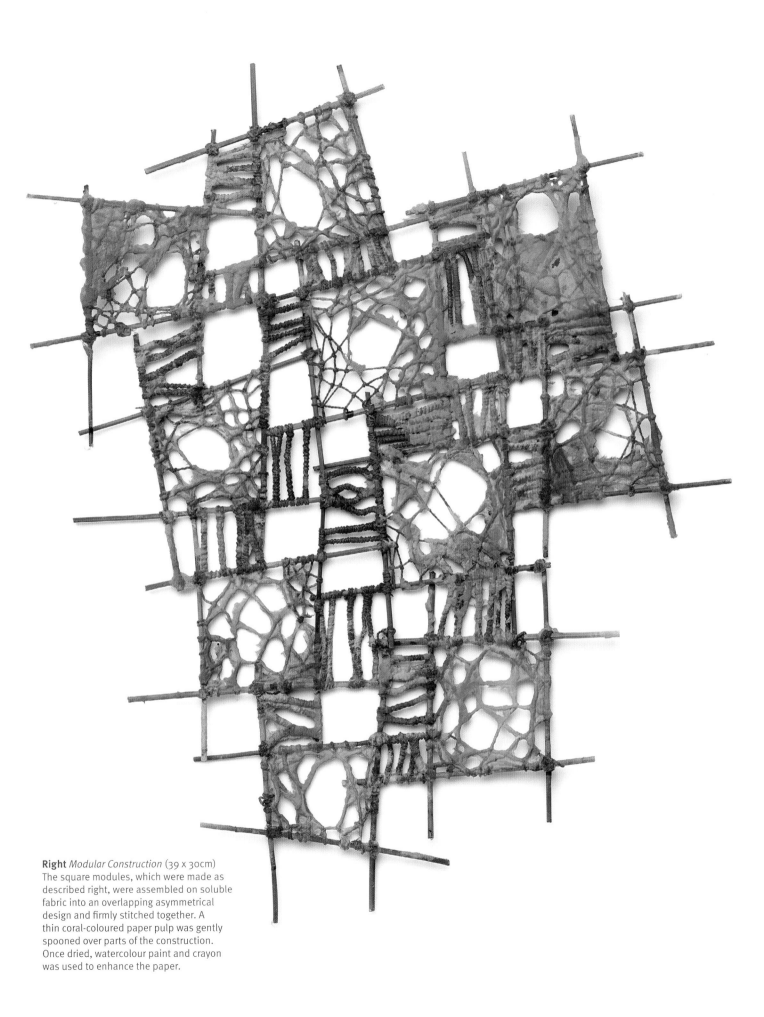

Right *Modular Construction* (39 x 30cm)
The square modules, which were made as
described right, were assembled on soluble
fabric into an overlapping asymmetrical
design and firmly stitched together. A
thin coral-coloured paper pulp was gently
spooned over parts of the construction.
Once dried, watercolour paint and crayon
was used to enhance the paper.

METHOD: USING ADHESIVE SOLUBLE FABRIC

REQUIREMENTS:
Adhesive soluble fabric; non-adhesive soluble fabric; sticky tape; cords and possibly other elements you wish to include in your construction; the threads you wish to use.

1. If required, your design can be firmly drawn on the reverse (white side) of the adhesive soluble fabric – the lines will show through to the sticky side. With the soluble fabric lying on a flat surface, carefully, little by little, peel back and remove the protective backing paper. Reserve the protective paper. See fig. 1.
2. Place the fabric, sticky side up, on a board. Fasten down corners and edges with tabs of adhesive tape. See fig. 2.
3. Place the elements and press in position on to the sticky surface. Ensure they touch, overlap or cross over each other consistently throughout the design. This is where they will be stitched together to form a strong, stable structure. If the design is a very complex one that cannot be completed in one work session, replace the protective paper to preserve the adhesive quality of the fabric and the positioning of the work. See fig. 3.
4. When the layout is complete, cover the whole surface with a layer of very fine transparent soluble fabric and press into place.
5. Begin stitching by joining the basic elements wherever possible so that the composition is all safely linked. Cords can be wrapped by stitching together, forming a wider block of stitches, or stitched more invisibly in a figure of eight manner. See fig. 5.
6. Additional wrapping, connected stitching and stitched fillings can be added, if wished. See some of the lacy stitched effects on pages 61–67.
7. Dissolve away the soluble fabrics. Drain and dry the work on paper towels.
8. Add further embellishments, if required. If the work is comprised of several sections, join together firmly.

SOLUBLE FABRIC AS A STABILIZER FOR COMPLEX CONSTRUCTIONS

In open or filigree constructions or larger, complex pieces of work, it is sometimes helpful to use the adhesive type of soluble fabric. If many elements have to be kept in place, they can be held in position on the sticky surface. I like to lay a fine, transparent soluble fabric over this initial layout to make it more pleasant to handle while stitching is carried out.

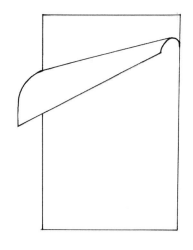

Fig. 1.

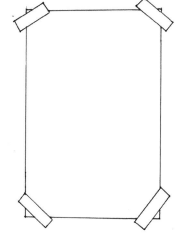

Fig. 2.

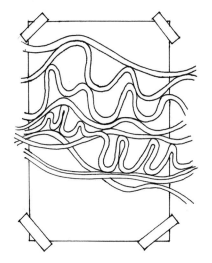

Fig. 3

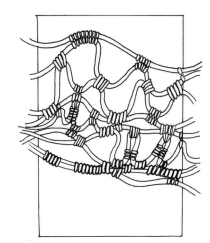

Fig. 5

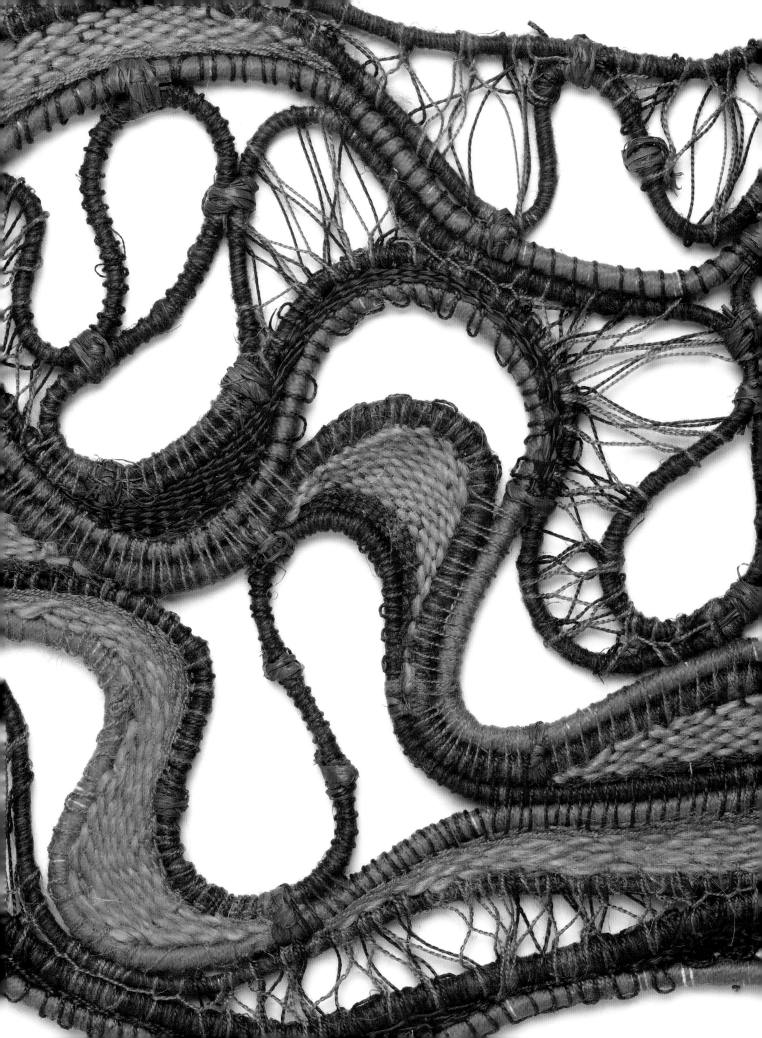

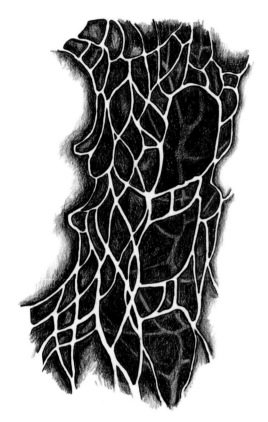

The orange piece pictured on page 73 was assembled according to the method described on page 72. Once the cords were firmly connected, in steps 3 and 5, the areas between were treated in the following manner to achieve strong contrasts within the structure. Lacy areas were made with Cretan stitch, while the solid areas were closely filled with weaving carried out over 'warps' stitched between cords (see page 67).

The tall three-dimensional works, *Cactus Form 1* and *Cactus Form 2*, shown opposite and based on the drawing left, were also made by the method described on page 72. Wrapped heavy cord was used to assemble the designs in long, narrow sections, to make it easier to hold whilst stitching. The sections, when complete, were stitched together after the soluble fabric had been removed. The work was very firm once joined, but I integrated long, wrapped willow sticks (or wires) into the design for extra stability. Space-dyed cotton thread was used to wrap the heavy cord and the colour was blended even more as the stitching progressed.

Previous page Sample using the method described on page 72.

Left Graphite drawing showing the detail of the complex lacy structure seen in a dried cactus.

Opposite *Cactus Form 1* (left) and *Cactus Form 2* (right). Both stand approximately 58cm high.

FURTHER STUDY: YOU COULD...

Practise hand stitching on different makes and thicknesses of soluble fabric, using the list of suggested stitches on page 60.

With the help of a good stitch book, try out other stitches. In conjunction with the ideas introduced here, many more innovative possibilities will be revealed.

Experiment with incorporating fabrics and other items into your work.

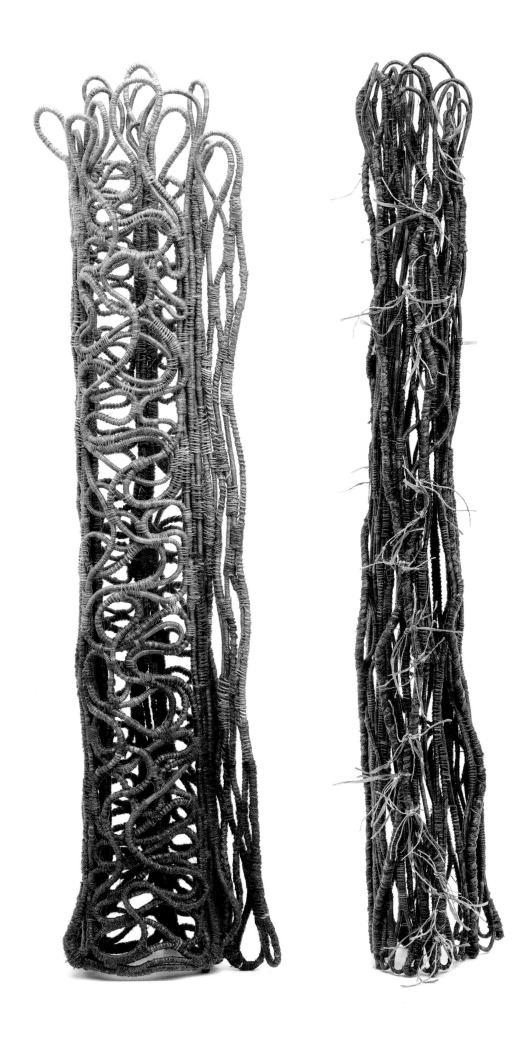

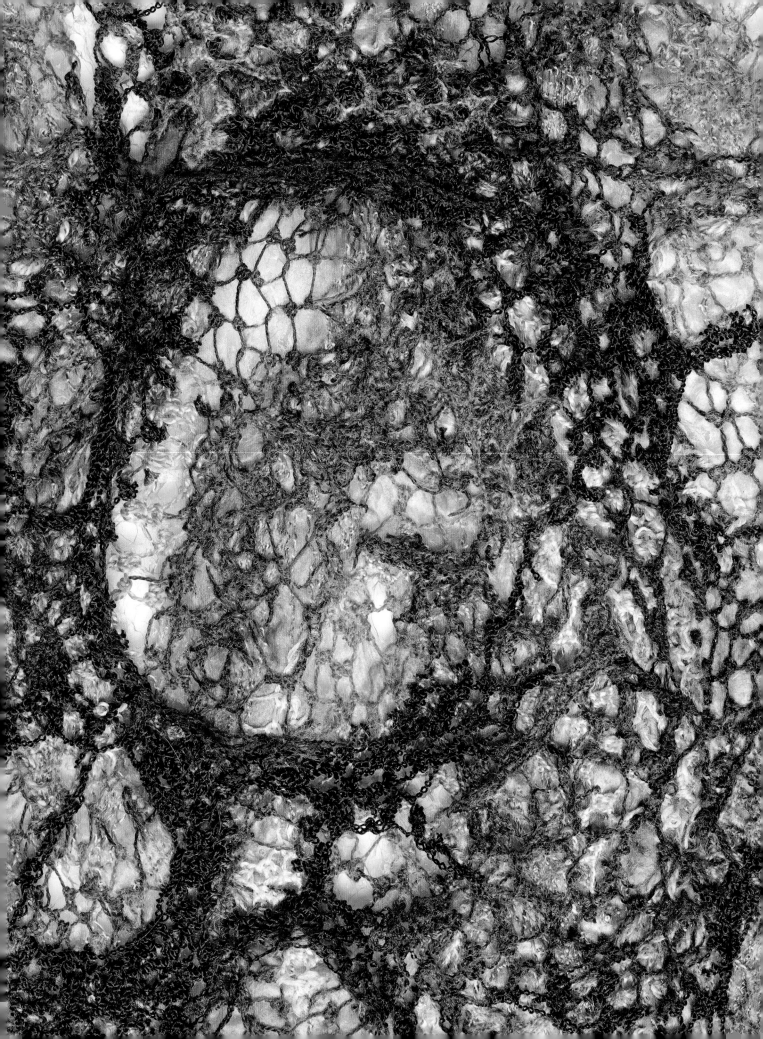

CONSTRUCTING WITH STITCH

Two- and three-dimensional stitched structures made without a background fabric. Making and using moulds for shaping stitched structures.

Opposite Detail of a small panel by Jenny Richardson. Fragments of chiffon were trapped between two layers of non-adhesive soluble fabric, then knotted buttonhole stitch, in small solid groups with spaces between, was worked in rhythmic, curving lines all over the piece. Density of tone and structure were achieved by layering the stitches. See page 82 for details of the knotted buttonhole stitch technique.

As mentioned in the previous chapter, some of the more unusual threads in my collection have enabled me to develop different kinds of work. My interest in baskets stems largely from studying the material culture of the peoples who have lived and worked in the landscapes that interest me. The work they made reflects both their way of life and the inspirational details of their environment, such as plant and landforms. Many hours spent travelling and in museums have led to much of my work, particularly to the small basket forms shown throughout the book.

This chapter is also concerned with increasing understanding of how a variety of structures can be made from stitch alone, without the need for a conventional background fabric. Some of the work has been constructed using the techniques described in the previous chapter and, in some work, mixed media has been included.

The structural quality of many of these lacy surfaces is emphasized and enriched by the shadows created by the work.

Essentially, in method, this work is based upon experiments grown from studying needle lace and stumpwork techniques, with the emphasis on a free approach and changes in scale of stitch and thread. The work of traditional and contemporary basketmakers has also been inspirational. The types of effect possible will largely depend upon the threads used, and it is important to experiment with as many as possible, including some you have made yourself and some of the less conventional types mentioned in Chapter 3. Structures made from stitch alone will only be stable if:

• The thread used has sufficient substance and stiffness to stay in place and/or
• The stitching is close and intense enough to make a firm surface.

You will notice that the structures illustrated here vary from very fragile to bold. Some work may need to be stiffened with a light coating of dilute PVA glue to give it protection and extra body but, because of the threads and stitch tension I use, I have not found glue necessary.

Above A soft lacy fabric constructed from a starting point of buttonhole rings (see page 84). Knotted buttonhole stitch was worked intuitively around the rings, which were gradually added as the sample grew. New thread was joined on and the direction of stitching was changed, as required, to complete the fabric. Cotton perle thread was used.

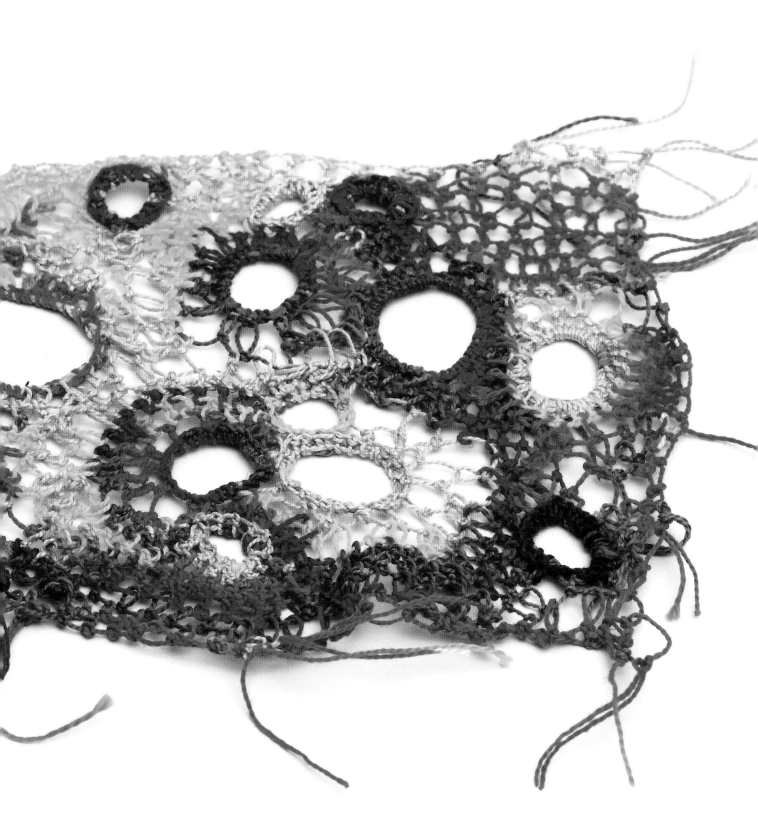

STITCHES

A variety of stitches may be used in the making of similar structures to those illustrated and it is worth experimenting with various stitches, using different threads, both alone and with other materials. Altering the scale and tension of a stitch gives additional scope. Initially, I have chosen to focus mainly on buttonhole stitch.

BUTTONHOLE STITCH

Buttonhole stitch, one of the most versatile and varied stitches in our repertoire, features strongly in much of my recent work and in the next set of illustrations. Traditionally used in stumpwork, buttonhole stitch still lends itself to many kinds of raised work with contemporary applications. With practice, you will be able to make both two- and three-dimensional structures, but as these are dependent upon thread type and tension, it is important to sample thoroughly before embarking on major pieces of work.

You will see from the photographs and captions that, as well as buttonhole stitch, other stitches have been used in my examples. These include: buttonhole stitch beginning with a buttonhole ring at the bottom of the form; knotted buttonhole stitch; weaving, and needle lace-type knots on crossed threads. All are made over polystyrene or rice moulds as described on pages 88–92.

Below Showing the contrasting possibilities when different threads are used, this sample was worked in exactly the same manner as seen opposite, top. The thread used here was a stiff dyed raffia, making it impossible to work the stitches closely. It was interesting to allow the thread to dictate the kind of open surface obtained.

Above A fragile surface made by working buttonhole stitch in a random, intuitive manner. New thread was joined on and the direction of stitching was changed as required to make a complete lacy fabric. Using the semi-translucent but crisp Japanese paper thread allowed for each stitch, separately, as it was worked, to be squeezed flat, so holding it in place. The three-dimensional forms shown right were made as a result of working this sample.

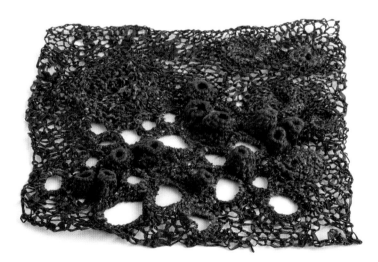

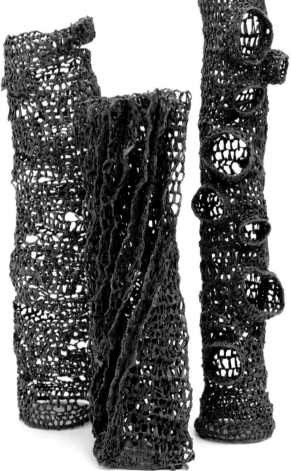

Above Three kinds of thread were used in this sample. The mounds were closely worked with linen knitting yarn in buttonhole stitch, starting with a tiny ring at the top. These were then connected by knotted buttonhole stitch worked in a soft Japanese knitting yarn, with more buttonhole rings in places. The final intuitive connections were made with a Japanese paper thread. Note the resemblance to the barnacle drawings on page 23.

Above Group of three fragile three-dimensional forms (heights 19cm, 23cm and 25cm) made in knotted buttonhole stitch with a fine Japanese paper thread. The forms were stitched over different cardboard cylinders to regulate the basic shape, before additional raised areas were worked on both the centre and right-hand forms.

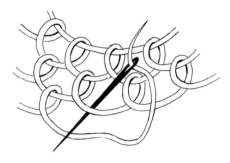

Working buttonhole stitch as a filling. Shown open for clarity but would be tightly worked.

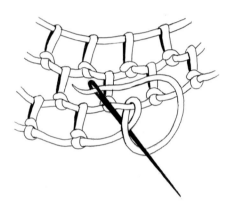

Working knotted buttonhole stitch as a filling.

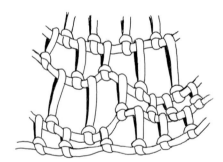

Knotted buttonhole worked in an irregular manner.

Right *Pinnnacles* (height 25cm). Three forms stitched in the hand in close buttonhole stitch with heavy cotton thread, and lightly touched with acrylic paint when completed. They were worked from the top downwards, increasing the number of stitches in each round, as needed. Thick cords, wrapped with synthetic sinew, and small beads were used as decoration. Each was finished with a tuft of horsehair.

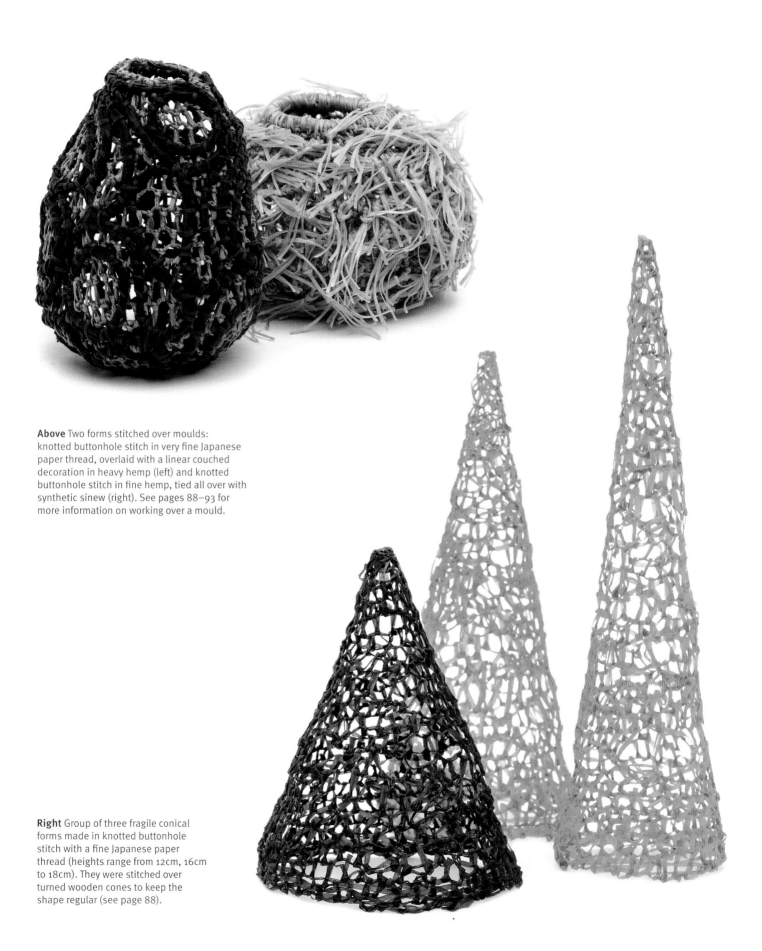

Above Two forms stitched over moulds: knotted buttonhole stitch in very fine Japanese paper thread, overlaid with a linear couched decoration in heavy hemp (left) and knotted buttonhole stitch in fine hemp, tied all over with synthetic sinew (right). See pages 88–93 for more information on working over a mould.

Right Group of three fragile conical forms made in knotted buttonhole stitch with a fine Japanese paper thread (heights range from 12cm, 16cm to 18cm). They were stitched over turned wooden cones to keep the shape regular (see page 88).

BUTTONHOLE RINGS

These can be made around one or more fingers, on wooden dowels and rods of different sizes, or on a couronne stick. Traditionally the latter was used in lace making and is small in size, but larger ones, made for contemporary work, are available too.

METHOD: MAKING BUTTONHOLE RINGS

REQUIREMENTS:
- thread of your choice
- a couronne stick or other wooden rod for working around
- tapestry needle

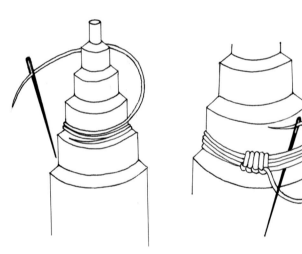

1. Wind the thread several times around the stick, in an anticlockwise direction if you are right-handed or a clockwise direction if you are left-handed (see fig. 1). Do not wind the thread too tightly.
2. Commence working buttonhole stitch, left to right if you are right-handed, or right to left if you are left-handed, over the threads around the stick (fig. 2). Complete stitching around the ring. Remove the ring from the stick and fasten off the thread neatly.

Fig. 1   Fig. 2

The two-dimensional work shown opposite is made from rings worked in a variegated cotton perle thread. This more delicate and formal style of arrangement was assembled using adhesive soluble fabric as a stabilizer, as described in the previous chapter.

The bold, white, lacy piece on page 87 was assembled in a different manner. It was made by working the large buttonhole rings, as described above, in a very heavy white cotton weaving thread that was quite soft in handle. These were then mounted on to Lutradur, a stiff, synthetic, non-woven fabric.

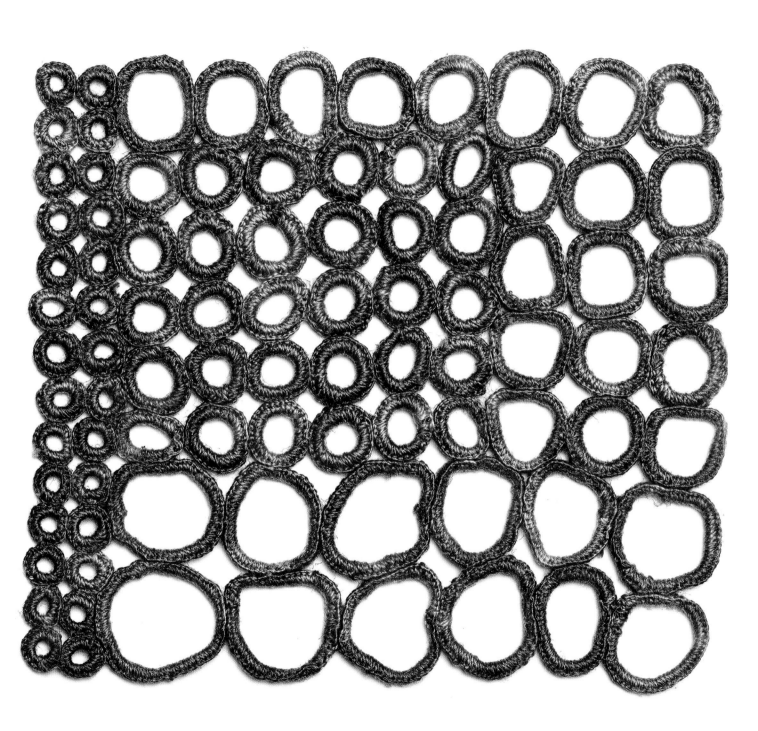

Above Formal arrangement of
buttonhole rings in fine space-dyed
cotton. See the method opposite.

METHOD: MAKING HEAVY BUTTONHOLE RINGS ON LUTRADUR BACKING

REQUIREMENTS:
- heavy cotton thread
- large couronne stick or other wooden rod for working around
- tapestry needle
- cord wrapped with similar thread
- Lutradur
- burning tool (soldering iron)
- acrylic paint
- respirator
- Please note – for health and safety reasons, a respirator is essential when burning materials

1. Work buttonhole rings as described in the method given on page 84.
2. Lay the wrapped cords on a large piece of Lutradur. Arrange the rings closely, distorting them as you do so to form an intense group. Leave a substantial border around the edges of the design.
3. Stitch or glue the rings to the Lutradur as invisibly as possible.
4. Wearing a respirator, use the burning tool to remove most of the Lutradur showing at the centre of the rings. This is achieved by burning a circle, which will allow the Lutradur to be removed. The slightly uneven edge of the hole gives a good contrast to the rest of the smooth Lutradur.
5. Mix water with acrylic paint to give a smooth, runny consistency. Carefully paint the whole of the piece of work, allowing paint to be soaked into the soft cotton of the rings. This will give them extra body and stiffness.

Opposite Relief panel made from buttonhole rings in heavy cotton thread, mounted on Lutradur synthetic fabric (size 30 x 28cm). See the method given left.

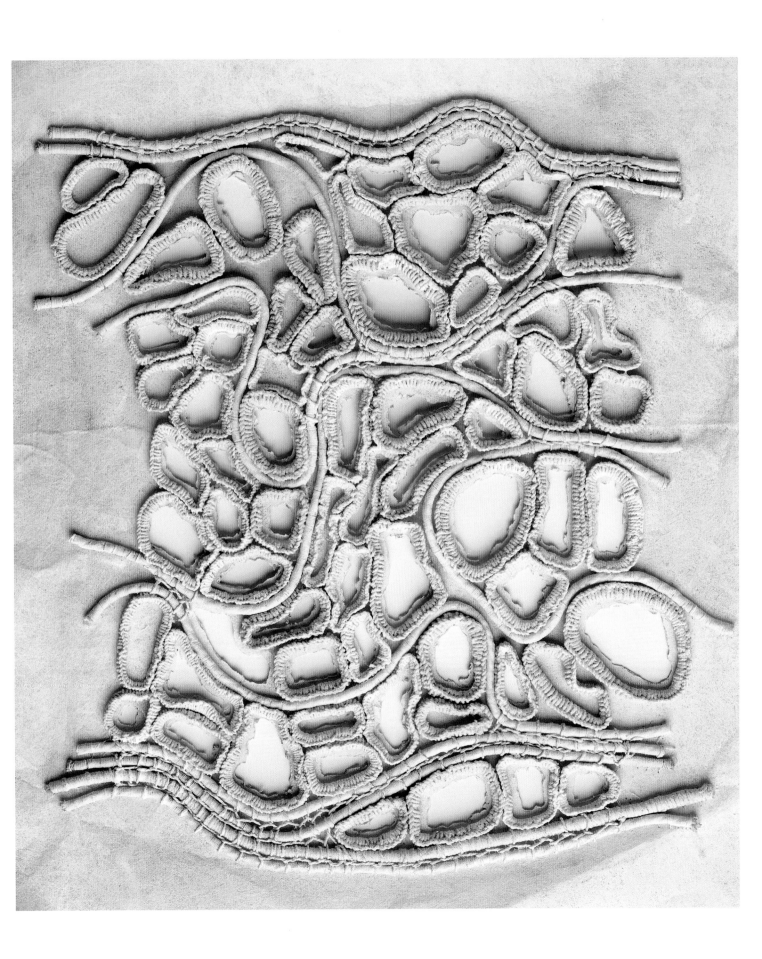

WORKING OVER
A MOULD

A wide variety of three-dimensional stitched forms can be made using moulds of different kinds, some of which can be readily improvised. The mould helps to shape the work well and enables a good stitch tension to be maintained.

To ensure the hollow structures worked over a mould hold their shape, it is essential to use substantial, sturdy threads, as described on page 78.

As mentioned earlier in this chapter, shaped wooden forms, thick wooden doweling and cardboard cylinders can all assist in shaping work. You will also find other materials to make improvised moulds. Polystyrene forms, available in different shapes and sizes from craft suppliers, make excellent moulds because work, during stitching, can be held in place with ordinary dressmakers' pins.

In making a hollow form over a spherical mould, it must be remembered that stitching can only go halfway over the mould (as far as the widest part) so that the mould can be removed. If an extended form is required, stitching can continue in the hands after the removal of the mould, shaping the work as wished.

Right Three small stitched forms made over moulds (made using the method described opposite). The threads and methods used were: weaving in very fine hand-spun Japanese hemp – method on page 91 (left); loose weaving in very fine Japanese paper thread – method on page 91 (centre); layers of knotted stitching (see page 63) in hemp and linen threads (right).

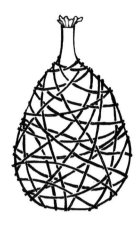

Step 3. Mould wrapped with sticky tape.

Step 4.

METHOD: MAKING YOUR OWN MOULD (DEMONSTRATED BY SHUNA RENDELL)

REQUIREMENTS:
- rice
- small polythene bag
- rubber band
- sticky tape
- thread with body and stiffness
- tapestry needle
- scissors
- tweezers

1. Place rice in a polythene bag. Squeeze firmly to compress the rice and to exclude air. Secure the top with a rubber band.
2. Flatten folds in the polythene and further compress the rice by tightly wrapping the shape with sticky tape, making a strong surface and a hard, firm form. Shaping is determined as the tape is wound around the rice-filled bag.
3. Wind sticky tape over the rubber band to make a strong seal at the top of the form.
4. Wrap thread around the form, weaving it alternately under and over previous threads as far as possible to make a stable and evenly distributed mesh.
5. Wrap the mesh with stitches, grabbing and pulling the threads together to form a strongly wrapped open structure. Gradually turn the work in your hands as you stitch. Continually assess all aspects of the form. Make sure the top edge of the form is firm and has a good shape. Additional weight can be given by darning the threads as in 5a.
6. Carefully cut through the tape and rubber band at the top of the form. Cut away as much as possible of the tape and polythene visible at the top.
7. Empty out the rice, then carefully remove the polythene and tape shell. Use tweezers, if necessary.
8. Adjustments can be made to the top edge if needed, perhaps with a row of firm stitching. If wished, make a ring of wrapped threads and stitch to the base of the structure to form a foot.

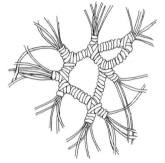
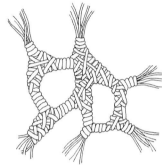

Step 5. Wrapping and darning threads together. Black sample.

Step 5a. Grabbing and wrapping foundation mesh threads.

Right Two forms, made over rice-filled moulds, in heavy linen thread (left) and heavy hemp thread (right). See above for method.

METHOD: KNOTTED BUTTONHOLE STITCH USED WITH A MOULD

Using your rice-bag mould (see method, p89) and starting with a small buttonhole ring pinned to the base (fig. 1), work knotted buttonhole stitch all over the mould, increasing and decreasing the stitches in each row as necessary (fig. 2). The stitches can be held in place with pins as work progresses. Once the top has been reached, and the rice and plastic have been removed (see instructions on page 89), you can work either a firm or decorative top edge (fig. 3).

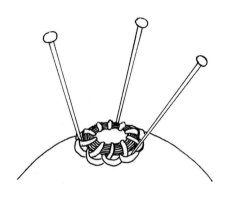

Fig. 1. Beginning with a buttonhole ring.

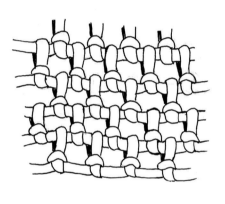

Fig. 2. Knotted buttonhole stitch.

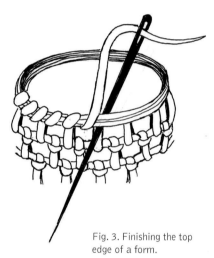

Fig. 3. Finishing the top edge of a form.

Fig. 4. Warp threads attached around the form and held at the top in preparation for weaving. Method described opposite.

Above Group of three soft forms, stitched over moulds with nettle fibre in knotted buttonhole stitch. The contrasting firm tops were stitched over plastic packing tape and decorated with synthetic sinew, small wooded beads and vintage, artificial flower stamens. The nature of the thread produces an irregular surface structure.

METHOD: WEAVING OVER A FOUNDATION OF WARP THREADS ON A MOULD

Make a small buttonhole ring and pin it to the bottom of the mould. Thread long pieces of strong, but thin, thread through the loops of the buttonhole stitches and secure these with a rubber band at the neck of the mould (fig.1 and fig 4, opposite). You will need a lot of these warp threads spread evenly around the form. Beginning at the base, proceed to weave over these threads until you reach the neck of the form. Remove the rubber band and mould as described in the method for making a mould (see page 89). Either leave the long ends of the warp threads as a decorative feature, or weave them back into the body of the form to fasten them off neatly.

METHOD: RANDOM OPEN HERRINGBONE STITCH OVER A THREAD FOUNDATION

Follow method on page 89 steps 1 to 4. Stitch densely in layers over the foundation threads, in tightly pulled open herringbone stitch. A firm surface can be achieved as in the small baskets shown opposite.

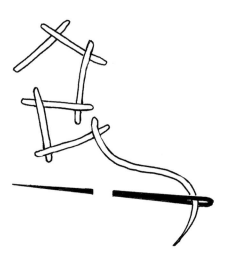

Irregular, random herringbone stitch.

Layers of irregular herringbone worked over a foundation mesh.

Form must be covered with layers of stitch.

FURTHER WORK: YOU COULD...

Practise a variety of stitches of different scales, densities and tensions with assorted threads, including some unconventional ones.

Try making different-shaped moulds and working over them.

Above Three small basket forms
made from Japanese paper and hemp
threads using the method described
opposite. They range in height from
8cm, 11cm and 13cm tall.

STRUCTURES USING STITCHED FABRIC

Making new surfaces from fabric. Using hand and machine stitching to transform the surface and character of existing fabrics.

Any fabric, woven, knitted or fused, has its own particular structure depending on many factors – the type of fibres used, the method of manufacture and the weight, flexibility and density of the finished product. While there is scope for interesting work made from all kinds of constructed fabrics, most of the examples illustrated here start from various types of woven fabric.

For some artists, weaving and the woven structure of fabric is the main focus of their work. Hilary Hollingworth, who is descended from a family of Lancashire weavers, references the creation of fabric in all aspects of her work. She uses the needle-weaving method to work into, and on the top of, an existing fabric to construct an exquisitely rich new surface. In the work shown opposite she has used this technique to depict fragments of her home landscape on felt. The warp and weft configuration of weaving, worked in fine threads made from newspaper, forms the basic structure for her design.

It is well known that fabric can be supported and stiffened with interlining or other material in order to create distinctive shaped forms, some examples of which are shown on the following pages. But the main emphasis in this chapter is the transformation, with stitching only, of the original structure of the fabric. Usually, this not only produces a new visual structure, but it also physically changes the character of the fabric, sometimes by creating greater fragility, sometimes by thickening, strengthening and perhaps creating a different raised, tactile quality.

My basic concept, when making embroideries, is to take a simple fabric, then alter and enhance it in such a way that it becomes my own new structured surface. In this chapter I have tried to explore and develop further the notion of structure in stitched textiles by using different fabrics and stitch methods.

In common with all my work, inspiration is derived from my drawings of natural forms and details from familiar surroundings. Most of the methods used to interpret my observations are my contemporary adaptations of traditional, recognizable techniques. As in previous chapters, both sampling of developing ideas and finished work is illustrated.

Changes to the fabric structure and surface can be implemented in various ways: it can be cut, folded, manipulated, layered, padded, scrunched, deconstructed and reconstructed. Stitching, by hand and machine, can supplement all of the above, sometimes only in a minimal way to hold the fabric in new shapes or, by contrast, richly in layers so that it completely transforms the original fabric. The latter – heavily stitching new structure into the fabric, thereby creating a dimensional quality – seems to be my natural way of working. See page 106 for an example.

In this chapter I focus on selected examples of the many ways in which fabric can be structured and re-formed.

Opposite *White over t'hedgerows* by Hilary Hollingworth. Weaving and darning in a variety of threads. See right for description.

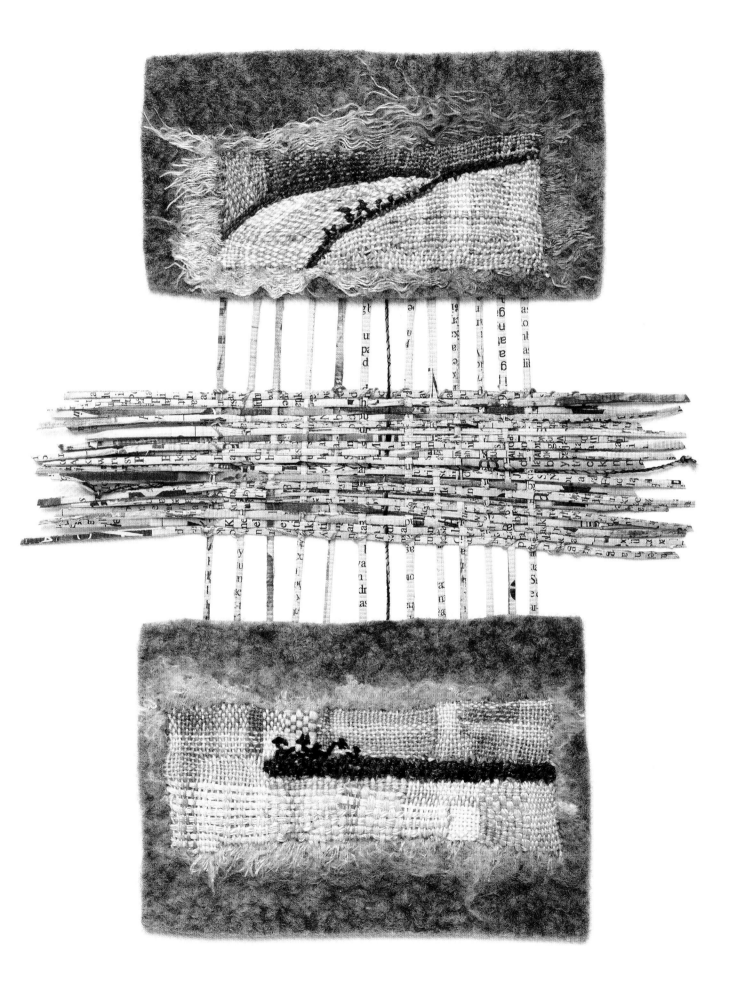

USING SMALL FABRIC ELEMENTS TO CREATE STRUCTURED SURFACES

Pieces of fabric can be folded, manipulated and decorated to make small modules such as dots, small squares, points and peaks. These can then be stitched together to form a variety of structural surfaces. Below, I show you how, beginning with a few open, lacy structures made from fabric squares.

The examples shown here demonstrate three different developments from one basic idea. The contrasting hard and soft edges and the changes in scale add interest. I have chosen to show these structural methods in the simplest form, using grids and squares, but many more shapes and complex designs are possible.

METHOD: USING SMALL PADDED SQUARES FOR AN OPEN STRUCTURE

REQUIREMENTS:

- small pieces of fine, smooth cotton fabric
- fabric scissors
- fine embroidery threads and embroidery needle or sewing machine and machine threads
- iron
- pencil and ruler
- adhesive soluble fabric
- thin non-adhesive soluble fabric
- mesh or sieve
- paper towels

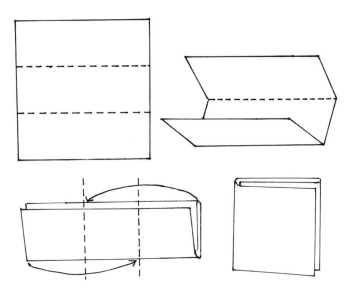

Fig. 1. Folding the squares.

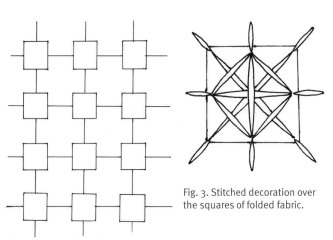

Fig. 2. Draw on the grid.

Fig. 3. Stitched decoration over the squares of folded fabric.

1. Make small neat squares of folded smooth cotton. Press to form crisp edges (see fig. 1).
2. Draw a grid on the reverse (the white side) of adhesive soluble fabric. Remove the protective paper from the soluble fabric as as shown in fig. 2 and work with the sticky side uppermost (the grid will show through). Carefully place the squares on the grid.
3. Place a layer of non-adhesive soluble fabric over your design to make handling the work more pleasant.
4. Join the squares with horizontal, vertical and diagonal lines of hand stitched running stitch (see page 61 for hand stitching on soluble fabric), carefully catching the corners of each square and making a large stitch across the square. In this example, the squares were further decorated by stitching an additional square on point. If wished, the squares could be connected with lines of straight machine stitching.
5. Rinse away the soluble fabric, supporting the work on a mesh or sieve. Stretch out to drain and dry on paper towels.

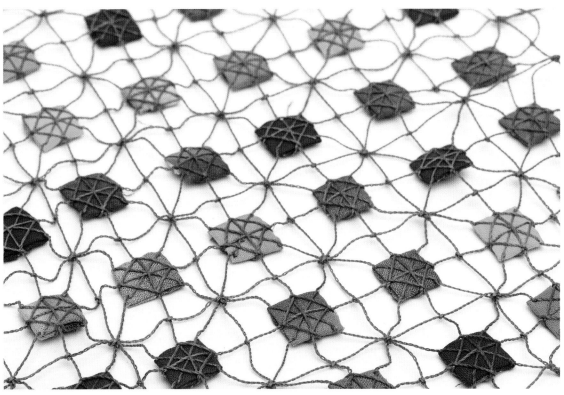

Left Sample of an open, lacy structure made from small padded squares, suspended in a mesh of hand-stitched lines. The slightly padded effect is a result of the several layers of folded fabric forming the squares. See method opposite.

Below Sample of an open, lacy structure made from softly frayed squares of fine fabrics, suspended in a mesh of machine-stitched lines. Some of the squares were cut on the cross grain of the fabric, allowing all the threads to be retained during the fraying process. See method on page 100.

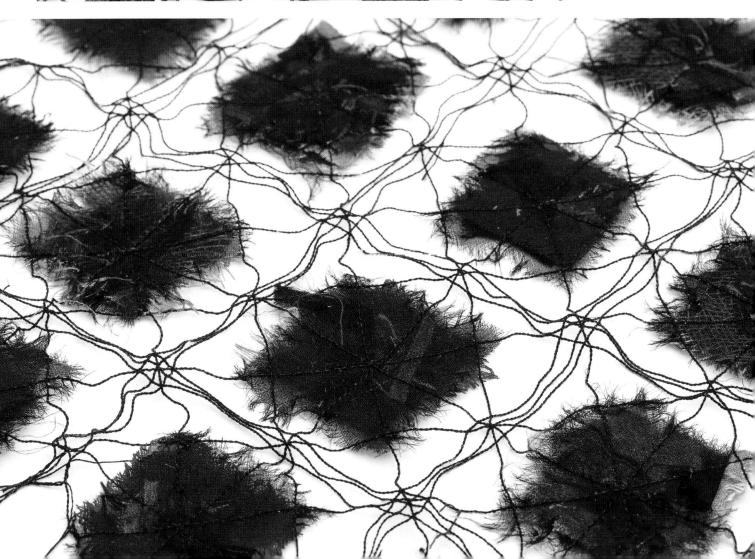

METHOD: A STRUCTURE MADE USING SOFT FRAYED SQUARES OF FABRIC

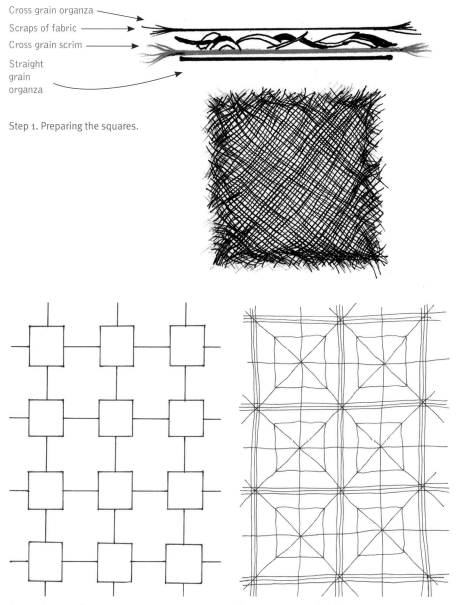

Cross grain organza

Scraps of fabric

Cross grain scrim

Straight grain organza

Step 1. Preparing the squares.

Step 2. Layout of squares.

Step 5. Machine stitching.

REQUIREMENTS:

- small scraps of fabric – organza, cotton scrim, silk
- sewing machine and machine threads
- fabric scissors
- pencil and ruler
- adhesive soluble fabric
- thin non-adhesive soluble fabric
- mesh or sieve
- paper towels

1. Prepare squares by layering fabrics. The example on p99 (bottom) has squares that consist of a backing of black organza, cut on the straight grain of the fabric, a slightly larger square of brightly coloured cotton scrim, cut on the cross grain of the fabric, small scraps of frayed fabrics in bright colours, all topped with a square of black organza cut on the cross grain of the fabric. The top two squares are distressed and frayed on the edges with the fingernails.
2. Draw a grid on the reverse (the white side) of the adhesive soluble fabric. The grid used for the example was 6cm (2¼in).
3. Remove the protective paper from the adhesive soluble fabric and, working with the sticky side uppermost, carefully place the layered squares on the grid.
4. Place non-adhesive soluble fabric over your design to make for easier handling.
5. Machine stitch (straight machining with the foot on the machine and feed dogs up) in the pattern shown.
6. Rinse away the soluble fabrics, supporting the work on a mesh or sieve.
7. Gently tease out the work to drain and dry on paper towels.

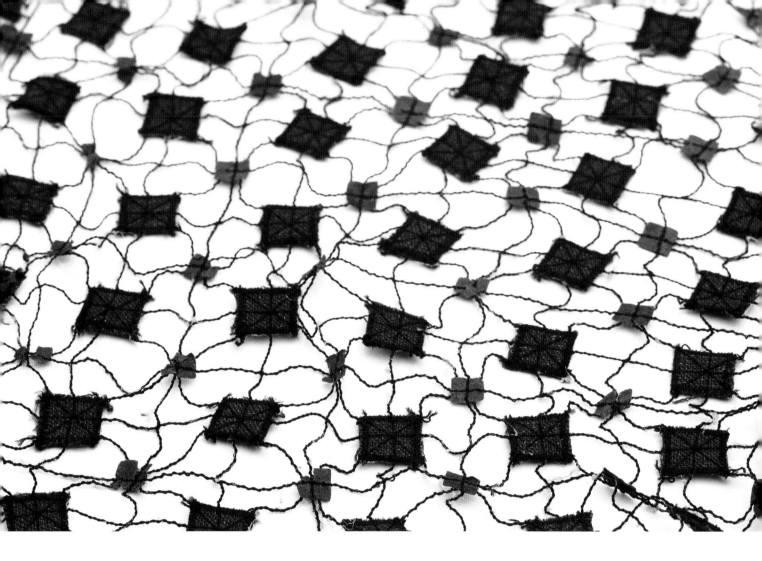

METHOD: DELICATE OPEN STRUCTURE MADE FROM ORGANDIE

REQUIREMENTS:
• cotton organdie
• sewing machine and machine thread
• very sharp small scissors
• pencil and ruler
• adhesive soluble fabric
• thin non-adhesive soluble fabric
• mesh or sieve
• paper towels

1. The example shown above is worked entirely by machine. Make the squares by stitching narrow satin stitch lines on the organdie in the formation shown.
2. With small sharp scissors, cut out the squares so that the satin stitch makes a firm edge.
3. From the spare organdie, cut more smaller squares with no stitched edging.
4. Prepare the adhesive soluble fabric as described above.

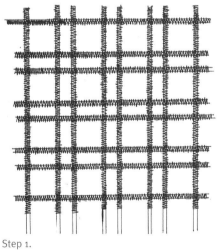

Step 1.

5. Position the squares on the sticky side of the soluble fabric. Lay thin non-adhesive soluble fabric over the design to make handling easier. Stitch in the pattern shown.
6. Rinse away soluble fabrics, supporting work on mesh or a sieve.

Above Sample of a delicate lacy structure made from tiny squares of cotton organdie, suspended in a mesh of machine-stitched lines. See the method given left.

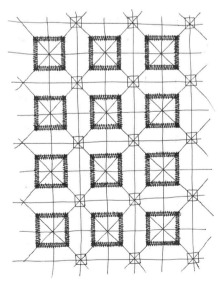

Step 5. Stitching pattern.

Several works in this section resulted from my observations of landscapes in the American Southwest after wildfires had devastated the vegetation. All the trees, the clumps of sagebrush and the cactus bushes were reduced to blackened stumps and, from a distance, the whole area seemed to be covered in black dots. Closer inspection revealed minute bits of colour were beginning to appear through the black, indicating regrowth. The two examples below and on page 105, and the works on pages 7, 117 and 125 show some of the other ways in which I have interpreted the aftermath of these fires.

METHOD: A STRUCTURE COMPOSED FROM HAND-STITCHED CIRCLES

REQUIREMENTS:
- smooth cotton fabric backed with matching felt
- embroidery needle and variety of embroidery threads
- narrow strips of coloured cotton fabric
- fabric scissors
- adhesive soluble fabric
- small pom-poms
- thin non-adhesive soluble fabric
- sewing machine and machine threads
- mesh or sieve
- paper towels

1. On the felt-backed fabric, hand stitch different sized circles with whip stitch (see page 120), adding rolled strips of cotton couched in place.
2. Carefully cut out the circles and place them randomly on prepared adhesive soluble fabric. Place the small pom-poms in the spaces. Cover with a layer of non-adhesive soluble fabric, pressed into place to cover the design and the remaining exposed sticky fabric.
3. Join all the elements with machine-stitched lines, allowing the machining to catch just the edges of the circles. Pom-poms can be stitched through. Ensure your machine lines connect all the elements.
4. Rinse away the soluble fabric, supporting the work on a mesh or sieve. Smooth out to drain and dry on paper towels.

Steps 1 and 2.

Left *Black Dots 1* (detail). Embroidered lacy structure composed of randomly placed circles in various sizes, and small black pom-poms. The circles were hand-stitched with whip stitch and couching, then all the elements were suspended in a machine-stitched mesh. See method above and whip stitch on page 120.

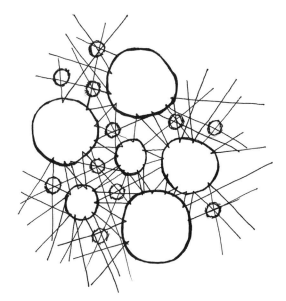

Step 3.

METHOD: A LACY STRUCTURE WITH MACHINE-STITCHED DOTS

REQUIREMENTS:

- adhesive soluble fabric
- small fragments of fabrics – cotton, chiffon, scrim, etc.
- fragments of mixed threads
- thin, transparent non-adhesive soluble fabric
- sewing machine and machine threads (or hand embroidery threads if wished)
- mesh or sieve
- paper towels

1. Remove the protective paper from the adhesive soluble fabric and lay it, sticky side up, on a smooth surface.
2. Randomly arrange small fragments of fabric and scraps of thread on the sticky surface to form dots of different sizes. In this example, some dots are all black others include fragments of colour. Allow ragged, asymmetrical shapes and edges.
3. Lay fine, non-adhesive soluble fabric over the design and press in place.
4. Freely machine over dots of fabric in dense circular rhythms. Join dots with running stitch (see page 62) or machine lines if wished.
5. Rinse away soluble fabric, supporting the work on a mesh or sieve. Smooth out to drain and dry on paper towels.

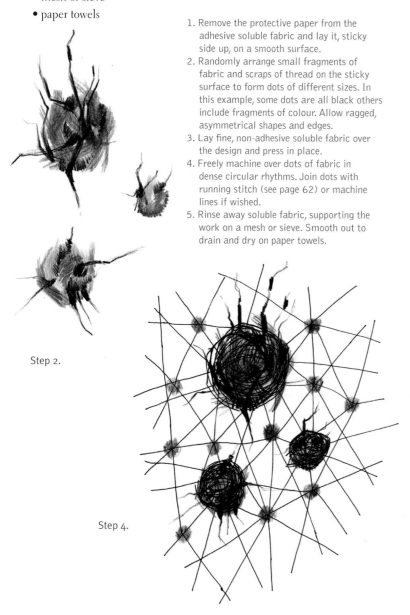

Step 2.

Step 4.

Below *Black Dots 2* (detail). Embroidered lacy structure composed of ragged, randomly placed dots made from fragments of fabric and scraps of thread. This piece was joined by lines of running stitch worked by hand (see p61) with knots worked where the lines crossed. Initially, too many lines were worked and later some were snipped away, resulting in the extra knots and notches on some of the threads.

METHOD: RAISED STRUCTURE WITH BOUND POINTS

REQUIREMENTS:

- small squares of coloured smooth cotton fabric
- embroidery needle and decorative threads e.g. cotton perle
- fabric scissors
- adhesive soluble fabric
- sewing machine and machine threads
- mesh or sieve
- paper towels

1. Grasp the centre of a square of cotton fabric and pull into a peak. Bind with sewing cotton to make a firm point.
2. Trim away excess fabric from the points, leaving a little to flare out and form a base. Arrange the points on a piece of prepared adhesive soluble fabric.
3. Join with free machine or hand stitching.
4. Add more decoration to each point by winding with heavier threads and stitching with overlapping long straight stitches and seeding to cover base.
5. Rinse away the soluble fabric supporting the work on mesh or a sieve. Lay on paper towels to drain and dry.

Step 1 (above and below)

Step 3. Hand- or machine-stitched lines to secure points to soluble fabric.

Step 5. Winding with extra thread and stitching the base.

Above *Large Dots* (15 x 15 x 15cm). This piece, part of an installation of large dots, was made with similar points. A polystyrene base was covered in black fabric and the decorated peaks were mounted all over it. The sculpture can be wall-hung or placed on a horizontal surface.

Left Sample of structure with bound points. The flat background was solidly hand-stitched with long straight stitches and seeding. See the method given opposite above.

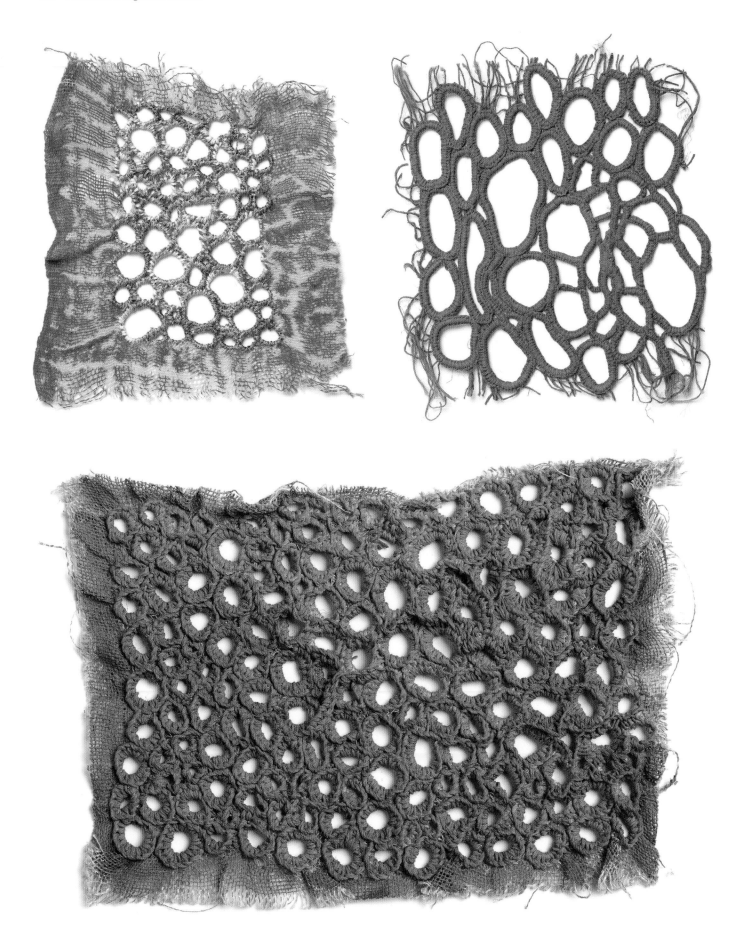

DECONSTRUCTING AND RECONSTRUCTING

A number of traditional embroidery techniques rely upon the deconstruction of an existing fabric that is then embellished and reconstructed with stitching to form a totally new fabric structure. Two such methods that can produce a variety of both delicate and bold open structures are pulled work and drawn thread embroidery. In the former, the tension of the stitches moves the fabric threads into new positions to form decorative shapes. Drawn-thread embroidery requires the total removal of some threads from the original weave, the embroidery being carried out on the remaining threads, sometimes regrouping them. Traditionally, fine evenweave linens were used, but for creative, sculptural purposes, any weight of fabric can be used, so long as the weave is loose enough for the threads to move easily. I find loosely woven linen scrim and the much coarser jute scrim particularly satisfying, because the thread grid can be readily distorted with the fingers, if required, prior to stitching.

The samples here show a variety of boldly stitched ideas. Note that care has been taken to change the scale of the work, creating different sizes of aperture and changes in the density of stitch texture. It could perhaps be interesting to experiment with overlaying some of these contrasting results for a multi-layered effect.

Opposite top left Sample of pulled-thread work stitched on cotton scrim. The holes were made in the fabric with the point of a stylus and then enlarged by easing the threads aside with the fingers. The edges of the holes were shaped and defined by over-sewing with a heavy variegated cotton thread. Note, very little fabric is left between the holes.

Opposite top right Sample of pulled work stitched on jute scrim. The fabric is very loosely woven and allows for very large holes to be made with the fingers. All the rearranged threads were covered in buttonhole stitch and, finally, the work was painted with clay slip.

Opposite Sample of pulled work on linen scrim. Holes were first made close together with the point of a stylus and were then stitched in closely worked buttonhole stitch, encouraging the purl of the stitch to stand high. This produced a rugged, raised, structured surface, which was then painted with clay slip.

Right The holes were made in the same manner as described above, but in this case they were much larger. The edges were closely stitched in buttonhole stitch with a smooth, fine cotton thread, totally covering the fabric.

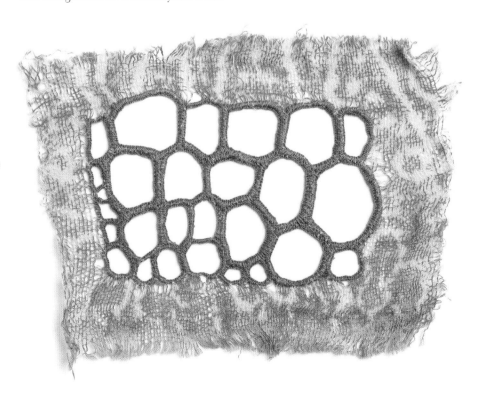

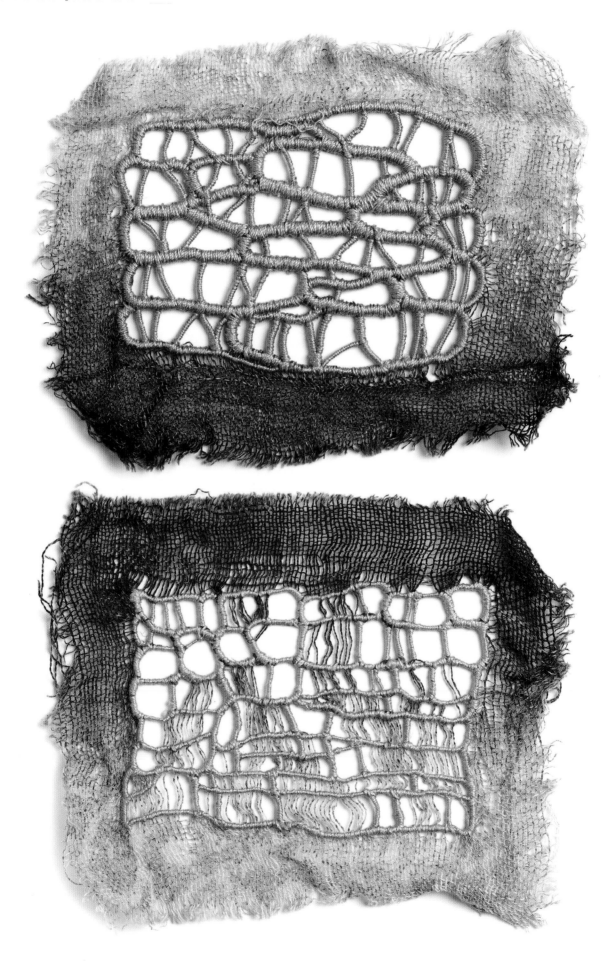

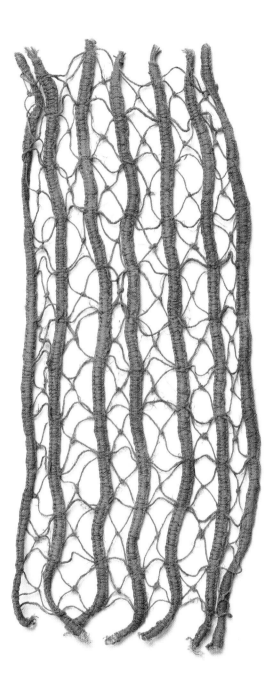

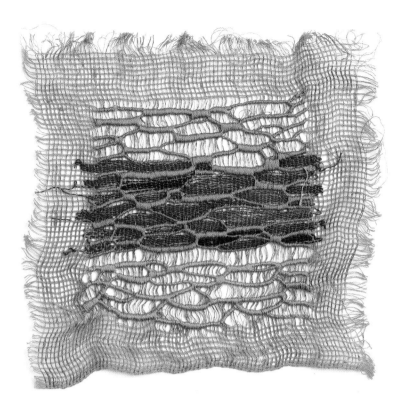

Above Sample worked on fine scrim. Some horizontal threads were withdrawn and a random linear structure was made by moving some of the remaining threads and closely over-sewing them with a silk thread. An area of the remaining vertical threads was re-woven with blue cotton thread, creating a new solid fabric.

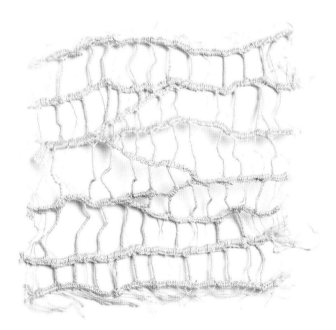

Opposite Two examples of drawn-thread embroidery. Some horizontal threads were removed and the remaining ones were wrapped in cotton perle thread. Notice the different appearance when the weight of the stitching is reduced in a similar design.

Above Sample worked on jute scrim with heavy cotton thread. Threads were withdrawn both vertically and horizontally. Heavy vertical lines were made by over-stitching the remaining threads with buttonhole stitch.

Above An experimental sample worked on a bleached vegetable bag. Threads were withdrawn both vertically and horizontally. The strong horizontal lines were worked in buttonhole stitch in a heavy cotton thread. Some of the vertical threads were wrapped with the same thread to create different weights of vertical lines.

LAYERS OF FABRIC

When fabrics are layered, one upon another, a new structure is created because the weight, thickness and handle, or feel, is immediately changed. Stitching on layered fabrics presents many exciting possibilities, perhaps usually associated with increasing bulk, often for practical reasons when resourcs are scarce or additional warmth is required.

However, beginning with the opposite extreme, fragile structures can be made by stitching shapes, or outlines, on to layered fabrics, areas of which can then be cut away to reveal those beneath. Very complex designs can be created, especially if, in places, the fabric is cut away completely, making open spaces.

The fragile work shown opposite, made by artist Wendy Cooke, is constructed from three layers of cotton organdie. The patterns in the design were derived from shapes observed while out walking; a good contrast in approach with some of the very textured works shown, which have similar beginnings. Wendy has used her machine with great precision to outline her design in narrow satin stitch, white on white, and has then cut through some or all of the layers, giving the piece a fresh, crisp, yet delicate appearance.

At the other end of the spectrum, stitching together layers of fabric to form a thicker surface immediately suggests the warmth and softness of quilting.

It is tempting to think of quilting only in terms of the refined, sophisticated hangings or bed furnishings that are so familiar. However, in many parts of the world, in order to conserve and recycle useful fabric, people have often layered old rags and scraps, using them to create a thicker, stronger textile with a much-extended useful life. Often, these textiles would have a great deal of stitching, which served both to hold all the layers and scraps together securely and also to decorate and strengthen the surface. Examples of this kind of layering can be found in patched traditional work clothes from Japan, in which more layers are gradually added and stitched into the surfac, by a method called Shashiko, as the garment wears. The inttuitively patched Gees Bend quilts from the American Deep South, also employed layered, recycled fabrics (sometimes unpicked, old work clothes) in their lively designs. Some Indian tribal textiles are composed of layers of rescued fabric (such as washed flour bags), including the kantha quilting from Bangladesh, which is especially important to me. This last method, in which several layers of old soft cotton saris are stitched together to give strength, produces a rippling surface of embedded stitching. My own work, shown at the end of this chapter, has been greatly influenced by this form of quilting.

Opposite *Cutwork Embroidery* by Wendy Cooke. The crisp, pared-back structure of this work is achieved by precise machine stitching and then selectively cutting the three layers of cotton organdie. See the description above.

KANTHA QUILTING

The exact form of the kantha is dictated by groupings of people and region. Although it is often described as a folk art, the work is complex in its diversity and also in the mythology and symbolism embedded in the designs. Here, in the consideration of structure created by stitch on fabric, I have not attempted to cover the method in its entirety. Instead I am simply describing my use of the basic running stitch to add structure to the layers of cloth and create the rippling surface so typical of the quilts.

REQUIREMENTS:
- very fine, washed (so that it is soft) cotton fabric
- pins
- fine needle
- embroidery thread such as very fine cotton perle

1. Stitching is carried out in the hands, without a frame. Make a sandwich from several layers of fabric. The number of the layers needed will depend upon the fabric, but four to five is probably workable. Tack the layers together to hold them in place.
2. Fasten thread on securely, then work rows of running stitch. The stitches should be smaller than the spaces between them. The tension should allow the stitch to be embedded in the fabric rather than lying loosely on top. Several rows of stitching must be worked before the rippling effect is achieved.
3. If the stitches are placed in an irregular manner, row by row, a random rippling effect is obtained. If they are placed in a regular manner below one another, ridges are obtained.
4. If the thread matches the fabric (see the samples right) the ripples tend to dominate the surface. If a contrasting thread is used, the stitches become the outstanding feature.

An artist for whom the kantha method has been very influential is Gwynneth Duffell, who has developed this form of stitching for her interpretations of the Australian landscape. Her layers are created by patching together quilting cottons to make a top layer over quilting wadding, and a bottom layer of cotton. After many hours of stitching, Gwynneth sometimes finishes her work by putting it in the washing machine so that the shrinkage that occurs adds to the surface structure of her work.

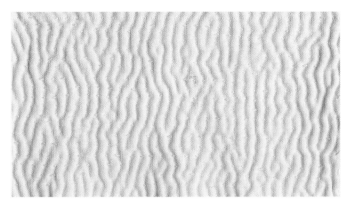

Step 3.

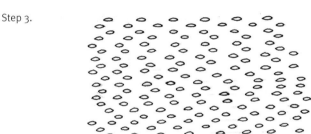

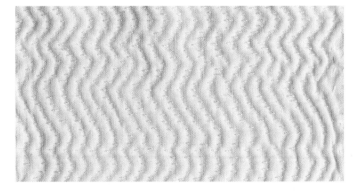

Step 4.

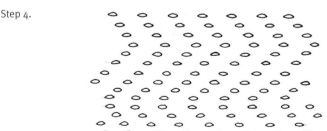

Opposite *Stoney Desert* (detail) by Gynneth Duffell. See the description left.

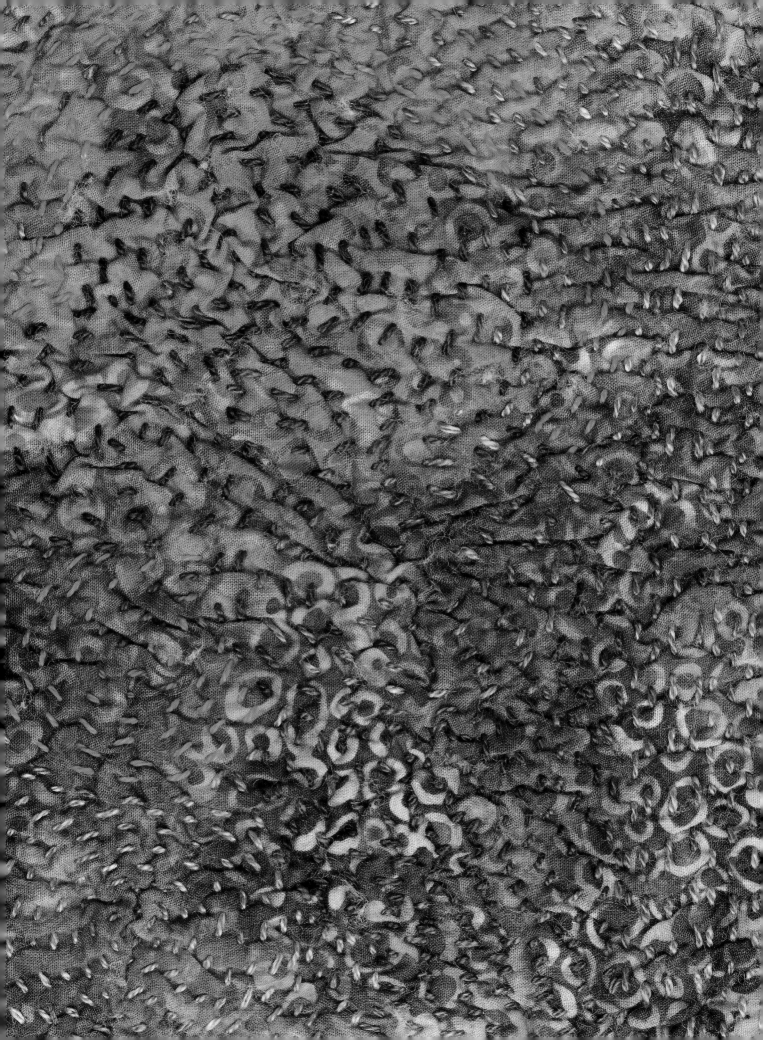

Right *Tall Rock Forms* (detail). Raised structured surface made with fine pintucks and exterior seaming.

Opposite, left *Tall Rock Forms* (height 79 to 86 cm). Group of three forms made from cotton with machined pintucks and hand-stitched seams. The work was dyed and painted when stitching was completed and was constructed over armature with weighted bases.

Opposite, right *Burnt Tree Forms* (height 66 to 76 cm). Group of three forms made from textured fabric with machined pintucks. The spikes were made by the method shown on page 106. Constructed over armature with slate bases.

MANIPULATING FABRIC WITH STITCH

Very simple plain fabrics can be given a completely new visual and tactile structure in a variety of ways, ranging from straightforward practical machining to intricate and labour-intensive hand embroidery.

Different forms of folding, pleating, tucking and gathering will change the structure of the fabric, producing manipulated raised surfaces. I have not attempted to expand on the numerous possibilities inherent in these methods, because they have been fully explored elsewhere by other authors and makers, but have simply chosen to show how I have manipulated fabric in my own work. The sculptural quality of these raised stitched surfaces is enhanced by the play of light upon them and, possibly, how they may fold and drape. To see how fabric treated in this way could be used, it is necessary to make large enough pieces for experimentation. Once a new fabric has been made, it can be used in the construction of many types of work, but is especially effective in three-dimensional structures.

Right *Burnt Tree Forms* (detail). Surface structure formed by machining pintucks in a criss-cross manner on a textured fabric. Acrylic paint was applied over the completed stitching.

My tall forms shown on page 117 are representative of megalithic rock structures, and are made from dyed and painted calico that I completely altered with close parallel lines of pin tucks, stitched on the sewing machine, using a twin needle. I have made many of these tall pieces and have experimented with different inner constructions, such as sculpture armatures, cardboard tubes and plastic plumbing pipes. Whatever support is chosen, it must be weighted at the base to give the work stability. It is best if the inner form is padded with wadding to provide a slight softness more appropriate for fabric sculpture. Additional shape can also be given to the tubular core with padding. The fabric was modelled over the core and hand stitched in place.

The spiky, tall forms shown above, inspired by the stark, remaining shapes of trees burnt in a wildfire, were constructed in the same manner. In this instance, however, the starting point was a textured fabric stitched with pintucked lines criss-crossing the fabric randomly. The spikes were made by the method described on page 106.

DEVELOPING WHIP STITCH

Over a long period of time, I have been interested in the surface textures and formation of rocks, especially where there is evidence of erosion (see the drawings left). Based on extensive looking and drawing, together with comprehensive sampling to find a way of expressing this subject matter, I have gradually developed hand-stitched work in which the fabric is totally restructured by the density and type of stitching used. Originally growing out of my appreciation and practice of kantha quilting (see page 114), combined with my experience of the manipulation of fabric on the machine, as described above, my work became more and more raised with complex surface convolutions. I found that, by repeating closely placed line after line of whip stitch, with a tight tension that pulled the fabric into ridges, I could create movement and rhythm on the surface. This could be even more exaggerated if the lines were made to twist and turn, or if they were set in groups at different angles. Colour could be blended and enriched by working back between the first stitches until, in some cases, the fabric on the ridges was virtually covered and became secondary to the colours and three-dimensional rhythms of the stitched lines. The work shown on page 29 shows the working method described.

Above Two watercolour drawings exploring the linear qualities of eroded rock surfaces. Drawings like these led to the development of the densely structured surfaces worked in raised whip stitch shown on the following pages.

Right Watercolour and ink drawing of sections of badly burnt trees, showing the crumbling, cracked surface structure of the bark.

These works, which I called rock fabrics, led to a series of pieces in which the same technique was used for stitching words. On seeing, from above, the layout of the walls of buildings in archeological sites, it occurred to me that they resembled lettering and I saw a way in which I could, perhaps, begin to use text relating to the landscape, which inspired the work. Although less dense in the use of lines of stitch, the surface structure of the fabric was completely changed because it was covered entirely with closely placed raised words. Worked freely on simple cotton fabric with cotton perle thread, these stitched textiles were sometimes painted with clay slip on completion. When dry, the slip was scoured with sandpaper to reveal the stitches and areas of fabric. The surface was then painted with acrylic wax to protect the slip, as in *Earth Quilt*, shown right.

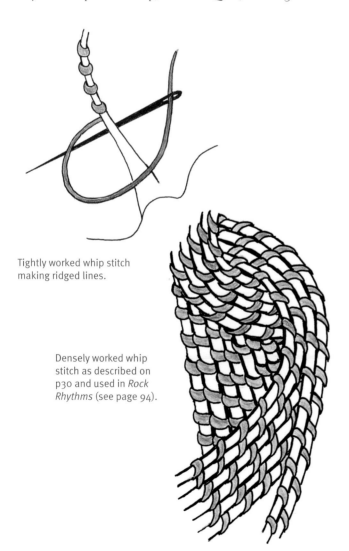

Tightly worked whip stitch making ridged lines.

Densely worked whip stitch as described on p30 and used in *Rock Rhythms* (see page 94).

Below Enlarged detail of *Earth Quilt* (see page 27 for full image), showing whip-stitched words that have been painted with clay slip then sanded to reveal the thread and areas of fabric.

Above *Three Arrowheads* (height from 11cm to 19cm). These three-dimensional structures were decorated in different ways: stitching inspired by kantha quilting with dried cloves on edges, painted with clay slip (left); rich surface stitchery with acrylic paint (centre); constructed over a mould using the method shown on page 89 and page 91 (right).

Below Pen-and-wash studies of arrowheads, showing a variety of shapes and surfaces.

Below right *Arrowhead* Three-dimensional structure with linear decoration in whip stitch.

Similar methods to those described above were also used in a series of three-dimensional work constructed from shaped pieces of stitch-manipulated fabric, representing details of the landscape. The arrowhead forms were, as so often in my work, the result of museum study and many drawings made of different arrow and spear points, which I find very beautiful and also tremendously powerful in shape, especially when bearing in mind their intended use. Referring to my drawings, I made a pattern of the proposed shape, then constructed it in stiff paper to see if it worked, making adjustments where required. A stiff interlining of either Pelmet or Craft Vilene, cut exactly to the pattern, was used beneath the outer stitched fabric, which was cut larger than the pattern to allow for turnings. The turnings of the outer fabric were folded over the interlining and firmly tacked in place. The two pieces needed to make the arrowheads were then placed wrong-sides together and over-sewn around the sides. For stability, a small weight was used to plug the aperture at the base.

Aftermath, a large, floor-standing installation, representing rocks, sand dunes and hills after fire, was made in much the same way, but each form consists of three pattern pieces. The base piece is cut from wood to keep these large forms rigid. The interlining shapes for the sides of the forms were covered in quilting wadding for a slightly softer surface. Making this work was physically demanding, both in the large amounts of outer fabric needed and also, despite their simplicity, in the amount of hard stitching required to construct and complete such a large group of forms (shown left).

There is no significant conclusion to this book because my work – research, drawing, sampling and making – is a continuing cyclical process, which I find to be always exciting and absorbing. By and large, although it has evolved gradually and logically from earlier influences, the work illustrated here spans just a few recent years. As I continue to investigate the notion of stitch and structure, new, but related, possible developments are revealed.

For me, stitching is a very physical process requiring energy, concentration and stamina. While it has to be accurate and controlled, it is not always necessarily dainty. I hope that having read this book, you may feel encouraged to broaden the scope of your own work in ways that are new to you. Also that you will enjoy discovering and recording inspirational structures, and go on to make lively, experimental samples and innovative finished stitched textiles of your own.

Left *Aftermath* (height from 22 to 48cm). Four elements of an installation consisting of seven forms, symbolizing the landscape after a wild fire. Three-dimensional forms made from cotton fabric which has been restructured with both hand and machine stitching. Mixed-media decoration.

FURTHER STUDY: YOU COULD...

Study and try out some of the methods described above.

Study and try out other traditional techniques that interest you including quilting, dyeing, basketry and stitching traditions.

Try developing your own version of some of these methods in response to the structures you have observed.

SUPPLIERS

Oliver Twists
202, Phoenix Road
Crowther
Washington
Tyne and Wear NE38 0AP
Tel: 0191 4166016. Fax: 0191 4153405
*Space-dyed threads; silk-paper thread; silk
and wool fibres etc.*

Habu Textiles
135 West 29th Street
Suite 804
New York NY 10001
USA
www.habutextiles.com
*Unusual threads and fibres from Japan,
including very fine paper threads.*

The House of Hemp
Beeston Farm
Marhamchurch
Cornwall EX23 0ET
Tel: 01288 381638
www.thehouseofhemp.co.uk
*Natural and dyed hemp threads in
various thicknesses.*

Mulberry Silks
Silkwood
4 Park Close
Tetbury
Glos. GL8 8HS
Tel: 01666 503438
www.mulberrysilks-patriciawood.com
*Silk embroidery threads of exceptional quality;
silk scrim; silk ribbon. Mail order only.*

The Silk Route
Cross Cottage
Cross Lane
Frimley Green
Surrey GU16 6LN
Tel: 01252 835781

www.thesilkroute.co.uk
*Wide range of quality silk fabrics: sari strips
Mail order only.*

Art Van Go
The Studios
1 Stevenage Road
Knebworth
Herts. SG3 6AN
Tel: 01438 814946
www.artvango.co.uk
Fine-art supplies, textile materials and dyes.

Barnyarns
Canal Wharf
Bondgate Green
Ripon
N.Yorks HG4 1AQ
Tel: 01765 690069
www.barnyarns.co.uk
*Large range of machine-embroidery threads;
soluble fabrics including Aquabond adhesive
soluble fabric.*

Texere Yarns
College Mill
Barkerend Road
Bradford
W. Yorks. BD1 4AU
Tel: 01274 722191
www.texere-yarns.co.uk
*Large range of plain and textured yarns,
including heavy linens and gimp.*

Ron Schmid
e-mail: ronandwendy@bigpond.com
*Australian craftsman in wood. Maker of small
and giant couronne sticks and other turned
shapes in interesting Australian woods. Will
mail abroad.*

FURTHER READING AND RESEARCH

Butler, Anne *The Batsford Encyclopaedia of Embroidery Stitches* Batsford, 1979
De Dillmont, Therese *Encyclopedia of Needlework* DMC Library
Greenlees, Kay *Creating Sketchbooks for Embroiderers and Textile Artists* Batsford, 2005
Haekel, Ernst *Art Forms in Nature* Prestel, 2009
Hedley, Gwen *Drawn to Stitch* Batsford, 2010
Jones, Richard *Nano Nature* Collins, 2008
Mitrofanis, Effie *Caselguidi Style Linen Embroidery* Kangaroo Press, 1997
Nordfors Clark Jill *Needle Lace Techniques and Inspirations* Search Press, 1999
Siegeltuch, Mark *The Thread Spirit* Fons Vitae, 2011
Snook, Barbara *Embroidery Stitches* Batsford, 1963
Williams, Christopher *Origins of Form* Architectural Book Publishing Co., 1995

Magazines:
Stitch The Embroiderers' Guild
Embroidery The Embroiderers' Guild

ACKNOWLEDGEMENTS

I am indebted to many people, especially my friends and family, but I give special thanks to the following: my sister Janet Read for constant support, encouragement and for proof-reading the manuscript of this book; my friend Doralee Wentsch who, on numerous occasions, generously invited me to stay in her home in Arizona and, over the years, drove me many thousands of miles showing me the American southwest; friends who kindly allowed me to use their work in this book; Margaret Chapman for invaluable studio help; Michael Wicks for beautiful photographs; Barbara Lee Smith for teaching me the coiling technique; and finally, the talented and enthusiastic participants in my Design for Stitch workshops in Lichfield, who continue to keep me on my toes as a teacher and maker.

Below A flexible structure made by trapping painted, wrapped flat sticks between two layers of transparent soluble fabric. The linking stitches were long lines of running stitch in fine cotton perle thread with a knot tied around each stick.

INDEX